ODYSSEY OF THE GODS

The History of Extraterrestrial Contact
in Ancient Greece

By Erich von Däniken

Translated by Matthew Barton and Christian von Arnim

New Page BOOKS

A division of
The Career Press, Inc.
Pompton Plains, NJ

ODYSSEY OF THE GODS
EDITED AND TYPESET BY DIANA GHAZZAWI
Cover design by Howard Grossman/12E Design
Printed in the U.S.A.
All photos by Erich von Däniken.

To order this title, please call toll-free 1-800-CAREER-1 (NJ and Canada: 201-848-0310) to order using VISA or MasterCard, or for further information on books from Career Press.

The Career Press, Inc.
220 West Parkway, Unit 12
Pompton Plains, NJ 07444
www.careerpress.com
www.newpagebooks.com

Library of Congress Cataloging-in-Publication Data
Däniken, Erich von, 1935-
    [Im Namen von Zeus. English]
    Odyssey of the gods : the history of extraterrestrial contact in ancient Greece / by Erich von Däniken ; translated by Matthew Barton and Christian von Arnim.
        p. cm.
    Includes bibliographical references and index.
        ISBN 978-1-60163-192-3 -- ISBN 978-1-60163-634-8 (ebook) 1. Civilization, Ancient--Extraterrestrial influences. 2. Greece--Antiquities. I. Title.
CB156.D332513 2012
938--dc23
                                                              2011027033

Contents

Preface

Do you know what an orgy is? Encyclopedias give its original definition as the celebration of religious rites in ancient Greece.[1] Nowadays the word refers to a much less restrained kind of caper, in which sex plays its fair share.

But in fact this is also what the word meant in ancient Greece. At that time, men used to meet together in the afternoon for philosophical debate, followed a few hours later by a "symposium" or drinking party—which often ended in an orgy. Wives were not present, but boys and youths were. Greece was taboo-free in this respect; people thought and felt differently in ancient Hellas.

Everyone knows what a science-fiction story is. But you probably don't know that there were science-fiction stories circulating in ancient Greece too, though much more fantastic ones than ours. The difference between them is that the Greeks didn't regard their science-fiction as utopian fantasies; they believed that the stories related events which had really taken place. And there was another difference. Our science-fiction stories—such as the adventures of "Starship Enterprise"—take place in the future, while the ancient Greeks looked back to a dim, distant past, to a time millennia before their own.

Just imagine that the island of Crete is continually circled by a metal guardian, which has the phenomenal ability to monitor all ships heading toward the island and to blow them out of the water. No foreigner has a chance of landing there against the wishes of the island's rulers. If a boat does manage to slip through, the metal monster can direct a fierce heat at it and burn up the invader. However, this guardian robot does have a weak point: if a certain bolt on its metallic body is undone, its thick blood flows out so that it is immobilized. Naturally, only those who constructed it, and their successors, know the precise location of this vital spot.

This story was already in existence around 2,500 years ago, and the Greeks were convinced that it told the truth about events long before their time. The robot which patrolled Crete was called Talos, and the engineers who knew the precise position of the place where the hydraulic fluid had to be drained, so as to inactivate the monster, were called "gods."

This ancient Greece is positively awash with incredible stories. In the *Argonautica,* a tale thousands of years old whose origin lies buried in the mists of time, so-called "centaurs" occur. What are they supposed to be? The "centaur" is a hybrid with a male torso and a human head—but the body of a horse. Basically an absurdity which should be a figment of the imagination. But hybrids existed elsewhere in antiquity as well. The historian and Church Father Eusebius (died AD 339), who also entered ecclesiastical history as the Bishop of Caesarea and an early Christian chronicler, wrote about it in Volume 5 of his works. "The Gods." Eusebius reports, "had created various hybrid creatures":

> And they begat human beings, with two wings; and then others with four wings and two faces and one body and two heads...still others with horses' hooves, and others in the shape of a horse at the rear and a human shape at the front...they also made bulls with human heads and horses with dogs' heads as well as other monsters with horses heads and human bodies...then all kinds of dragon-like monstrous beings...of many kinds and different from one another, whose images they kept in the Temple of Belus depicted one next to the other....[2]

"Human beings with two wings" are said to have existed? Nonsense? Why, then, do their reliefs stare out at us from steles and sculptures in all major museums? The only difference is that they are not called "human beings with two wings" because our modern archeology refers to them as "winged genii." "Human beings with horses' hooves"—centaurs—half man half horse, are immortalized in images from antiquity. And they are said to have created "bulls with human heads." The Cretan monster, the

Minotaur, was one such monstrosity. A bull with a human head for which the Cretans had the famous Labyrinth built.

Could it be, then, that the ancient stories in the *Argonautica* are not fairy tales at all? Are they accounts of real events? And when in the endless river of time is all this supposed to have happened?

No one knows. But there is a temple in Malta which has been dated by specialists to 12,000 BC on the basis of its astronomical orientation. And there are underwater sites both in the Atlantic and the Pacific. In the Mediterranean, not far from Marseilles, divers discovered an underwater tunnel at a depth of 35 meters with an upward incline. The tunnel led into a 40-meter-long corridor and ended in a lake. At the surface of the lake, the torches illuminated a picture gallery: C-14 samples from the colors produced an age of about 18,000 years.

There appears to be something not quite right with our dating. Are the Greek tales much older than the research is prepared to admit? Could it be that they—or at least some of them—are not inventions at all, classical "science fiction," but that they represent a reality of the past?

This is not a (hi)story book of ancient Greece, but a book about its stories. The Greece of ancient times is chockablock with extraordinary tales. Did the wanderings of Odysseus ever happen? What was going on in Delphi? Was there really a doom-and-gloom prophetess there who foresaw all major political events? Are the powerful descriptions of Troy based on truth? And what about Atlantis? All the information we have about Atlantis, to which all authors on the subject refer, has come from Greece. And who were the Argonauts who set out to steal the "Golden Fleece"?

Greece is worth exploring. I invite you to join me on a special kind of adventure.

Chapter 1

Adventures of the Starship Enterprise in Long-Gone Millennia

Impure means lead to an impure end.

—Mahatma Gandhi, 1869–1948

A long, long time ago there lived a distant descendant of the gods. No one knows his original name, but the Greeks called him Jason. I'll have to make do with this name since I don't know any other. Now Jason was no ordinary man, for blue blood ran in his veins. His father was King Aison of Iolchos in Thessalia. But, as so often in mythology, Jason had a wicked stepbrother who deprived him of the throne when he was still an infant. Jason's father arranged for his small offspring to be brought up by a centaur. Others say that it was his mother who took him to the centaur, but that is not the important thing here.[1, 2] The centaurs were a curious cross-breed, with a man's head and upper torso and arms, but the body of a horse. A truly astonishing phenomenon. And Jason must have had a rather unusual kind of upbringing!

Jason is connected with an oracle, for anyone who was anything in ancient Greece had something to do with an oracle. The prophecy in this case warned of a man with just one sandal. As the disreputable king, Jason's stepbrother was one day holding a celebratory buffet on the beach, when a tall, beautiful young man came striding along. This was Jason, and he was wearing only one sandal because he had lost the other in the mud of a river. Jason was clothed in a leopard's skin and a leather tunic. The king did not recognize the stranger and asked irritably who he was. Jason, smiling, answered that his foster-father the centaur called him Jason, but that his real name was Diomedes, and he was the son of King Aison.

Jason soon realized with whom he was talking, and quickly demanded the throne back, which was rightfully his. Surprisingly the king agreed, but on one condition—which, he assumed, could not be fulfilled. He said that Jason must free his kingdom from a curse, which had been laid both on him and on the whole country. He must fetch the Golden Fleece that was guarded by a dragon in a faraway place. This dragon never slept. Only when this deed had been accomplished would the king relinquish his kingdom.

Jason agreed, and thus began the most incredible science-fiction story. First, Jason went in search of an extraordinary shipbuilder, who would construct the most amazing ship of all time. This man was called Argos, and scholars disagree about where he came from. What is certain is that Argos must have been an outstanding engineer, for he built Jason a ship unlike any that had ever been seen before. Naturally, Argos had unusual connections, for none other than Athene herself gave him advice, and under her direction a vessel was built from a kind of wood which "never rots."[3] Not content with that, Athene personally contributed an unusual sort of beam and built this in to the ship's bows. It must have been an astonishing piece of wood, for it could speak. Even as the ship left the harbor, the beam shouted out in gladness because the journey was starting, and later it warned the ship's company of many dangers. Argos, the shipbuilder, christened the mighty ship Argo, which in ancient Greek means roughly "fast" or "fleet-footed."[4] The ship's company were thus called "Argonauts," and the whole story is called the *Argonautica*. (Our astronauts and cosmonauts take their name indirectly from the Greek Argonauts.)

The Argo had room for 50 men, who must all have been specialists in various fields. That is why Jason had sent messages to every royal house in his search for a team of volunteers with particular abilities. And they came, all heroes and offspring of the gods. The list of the original crew is only partially preserved, and scholars say that other names were added by later authors.[5, 6, 7] The crew must have been quite phenomenal, and it included the following people: Melampus, a son of Poseidon; Ancaeus of Tegeg, also a Poseidon offspring; Amphiarus the seer; Lynceus the look-out; Castor of Sparta, a wrestler; lphitus, the brother of the king of Mycenae; Augeias, the son of the king of Phorbas; Echion the herald, a son of Hermes; Euphemus of Tainaron, the swimmer; Heracles of Tiryns, the strongest man; Hylas, the beloved of Heracles; Idmon the Argive, a son of Apollo; Acastus, a son of King Pelias; Calais, the winged son of the Boreas; Nauplius, the sailor; Polydeuces, the prizefighter from Sparta; Phalerus, the archer; Phanus, the Cretan son of Dionysus; Argos, the builder of the Argo; and Jason himself, the leader of the enterprise.[8, 9]

The various authors who described the journey of the Argo more than 2,000 years ago added other names. At different points in Greek history, writers or historians concerned with the Argonauts assumed that this or that famous character must also have been there. The oldest list is in the Pythian Poem IV, recorded by a writer called Pindar (roughly 520–446 BC). This contains only ten names: Heracles, Castor, Polydeuces, Euphemnus, Periclymenus, Orpheus, Echion, and Eurytus (both sons of Hermes, the messenger of the gods), as well as Calais and Zetes. [10, 11] Pindar continually emphasizes that all these heroes were of divine descent.

The best and also most detailed description both of the whole journey and the heroes taking part in it, comes from Apollonius of Rhodes. He lived at some point between the 3rd and 4th centuries BC. Now Apollonius was certainly not the originator of the *Argonautica*. Various scholars assume that he must have drawn the basic story from much older sources.[12, 13] Apollonius writes in his "First Song" that poets before him had told how Argos, guided by Pallas (Athene), had built the ship. Fragments of the *Argonautica* can be traced back as far as the 7th century BC. Scholars do not exclude the possibility that the story actually originated in ancient Egypt.

The *Argonautica* by Apollonius was translated into German in 1779. In quoting from the story, I will mainly draw upon this translation, now over 200 years old. The 1779 translation is not yet imbued with our modernist attitudes, and reflects Apollonius' original flowery style. An excerpt from the list of names, written down roughly 2,400 years ago, goes as follows:

> Polyphemus, the Elatid, came from Larissa. Long ago he had stood shoulder to shoulder with the Lapiths, fighting in battle against the wild centaurs...

Mopsus came too, the Titaresian, who had learned from Apollo to interpret the flight of birds...

Iphitus and Clytias were also of his party, the sons of wild Eurytus, to whom the god who shoots far had given the bow...

Alcon had sent his son, although no son now remained in his house...

Of the heroes who left Argos[14] Idmon was the last. He learned from the god [Apollo] the art of watching the flight of birds, of prophecy and of reading the meaning of the fiery meteors...

Lynceus came also...his eyes were unbelievably sharp. If the rumor is true, he could see deep into the earth...

Afterwards came Euphemus from the walls of Tenaros, the most fleet of foot... two other sons of Neptune came too....[15]

Whichever list of names is closest to the original, the Argonauts were, at any rate, a hand-picked company of gods' sons, each with his own astonishing gifts and special expertise. This extraordinary group gathered in the harbor of Pagasai on the Magnesia peninsula, to set off with Jason in his quest for the Golden Fleece.

Before the journey began, they held a feast in honor of Zeus, the father of the gods,[16] and then the whole team marched on board, through a crowd of thousands of inquisitive observers. Apollonius describes it as follows:

Thus did the heroes pass through the town and make their way down to the ship.... With them and around them ran a great, foolish mob. The heroes shone like stars in the sky between the clouds...[17]

The people hailed the brave seafarers and wished them success in all their undertakings and a safe homecoming, while anxious mothers pressed their children to their breasts. The whole town was in uproar until the Argo finally sailed over the horizon and vanished from sight.

And why all this effort? Because of the Golden Fleece. But what is this slightly bizarre object of desire? Most encyclopedias I consulted describe the Golden Fleece as the "fleece of a golden ram."[18, 19, 20, 21] So this whole

Argonaut crew is supposed to have set sail because of a fleece? The greatest ship of the time is supposed to have been built, and sons of gods and kings to have freely offered their services, in the quest of a ridiculous bit of fur? And a curse—one that needed such effort to combat—was supposed to hang over the country because of this? And a dragon, who "never sleeps," was meant to guard this lousy fleece day and night. Surely not!

No, definitely not, for the Golden Fleece was a very particular skin with astonishing properties. It could fly!

The legend tells that Prixos, a son of King Athamas, had suffered a great deal because of his wicked stepmother, until his real mother snatched him and his sister away. She placed the children on the back of a winged golden ram, which the god Hermes had once given her, and on this miraculous beast the two flew through the air over land and sea, finally landing in Aia, the capital of Colchis. This was a kingdom at the farthest end of the Black Sea. The king of Colchis is described as a violent tyrant who easily broke his word when it suited him, and who wanted to hang on to this "flying ram." The Golden Fleece was thus nailed firmly to a tree. In addition, the services of a fire-spitting dragon which never slept were enlisted to guard it.

So the Golden Fleece was some kind of flying machine that had once belonged to the god Hermes. It must on no account remain in the hands of a tyrant, who might have misused it for his foul purposes—hence the top-class crew with their various expertise, and the help of the gods' descendants. They all wanted to regain what had been the property of the Olympians.

Hardly had they embarked when the Argonauts elected a leader in democratic manner. Heracles, the strongest of all men, was chosen, but he turned down the job. He declared that this honor belonged to Jason alone, the initiator of the whole expedition. The ship passed swiftly out of Pagasai harbor and rounded the peninsula of Magnesia.

After a few harmless adventures, the crew reached the Capidagi peninsula, which is connected to the mainland by a strip of land. There lived the Dolion people, whose young king Cyzicus asked the Argonauts to tie up in the harbor in the bay of Chytos—somehow forgetting to warn them about the giants with six arms who also lived there. The unsuspecting Argonauts climbed a nearby mountain to get their bearings.

Only Heracles and a few men remained to guard the Argo. The six-armed monsters immediately attacked the ship—unaware, however, of Heracles, who saw them coming and killed a few of them with his arrows before the battle even began. Meanwhile the other Argonauts returned, and thanks to their special talents, butchered the attackers. Apollonius writes of these giants: "Their body has three pairs of sinewy hands, like paws. The first pair hangs on their gnarled shoulders, the second and third pairs nestle at their horrible hips..."[22]

Giants? Nothing more than the fantasy of a story-teller? In our forefathers' ancient literature, at least, such beings are not uncommon Any Bible reader will remember the fight between David and Goliath. And in Genesis it says: "There were giants in the earth in those days, and also after that, when the sons of God came in unto the daughters of men, and they bare children to them...."[23]

Other passages in the Bible which speak of giants are Deuteronomy 3:3-11; Joshua 12:4; 1 Chronicles 20:4-5; Samuel 2 1:16. And in the book of the prophet Enoch there is an extensive description of giants. In Chapter 14 one can read: "Why have you done as the children of earth and brought forth the Sons of giants?"[24]

In the Apocrypha of Baruch we even find numbers: "The Highest brought the flood upon the earth, and did away with all flesh and also the 4,090,000 giants."[25] This is confirmed in the *Kebra Negest*, the story about the Ethiopian kings:

> Those daughters of Cain, however, with whom the angels had done indecent acts, became pregnant, but could not give birth, and died. And of those in their wombs, some died and others came out by splitting the bodies of their mothers...as they grew older and grew up these became giants.[26]

And in the books containing the "tales of the Jews in ancient times"[27] one can even read about the different races of these giants. There were the "Emites" or "Frightful Ones," then the "Rephaites" or "Gargantuans"; there were the "Giborim" or the "Mighty Ones," the "Samsunites" or the "Sly Ones"; and finally the "Avides" or "Wrong Ones" and the "Nefilim" or "Spoilers." And the book of Eskimos is quite certain on this point: "In those days there lived giants on the earth."[28]

I could carry on quoting such passages, but I would prefer not to repeat material from earlier books. Giants' bones have also been found, although some anthropologists still try to insist that these are the bones of gorillas.[29] In 1936 the German anthropologist Larson Kohl discovered the bones of giant people on the shores of the Elyasi Lake in Central Africa. The German paleontologists Gustav von Königsberg and Franz Weidenreich were astonished to find several giants' bones in Hong Kong chemists' shops in 1941. The discovery was published and scientifically documented in the American Ethnological Society's annual report of 1944.

About 3.5 miles (6 km) from Safita in Syria archaeologists dug up hand axes which could only have been used by people with giant hands. The stone tools which came to light in Ain Fritissa (East Morocco), measuring 12.5 × 8.5 inches (32 × 22 cm), must also have belonged to some hefty people. If they were able to wield such tools, which weigh up to 9.5 pounds (4.3kg), they must have been over 13 feet (4 m) tall. The discoveries of giants' skeletons in Java, South China, and Transvaal (South Africa) are well known from specialist literature. Both Professor Weidenreich[30] and Professor Saurat[31] carefully documented their scientific research into giants. And the former French representative of the Prehistorical Society, Dr. Louis Burkhalter, wrote in the 1950 edition of the Revue du Musee de Beyrouth: "We want to make clear that the existence of giant people [in ancient times]...must be regarded as a scientifically certain fact."

The *Epic of Gilgamesh* from Sumeria also tells of giants, as does, at the other end of the world, the Popol Vuh of the Mayans. The Nordic and Germanic myths, too, are peopled by giants. So why would the ancient world have so many stories about beings who never existed?

Image 1: The Gigantia temple on the Mediterranean island of Gozo is of unknown date.

Image 2: Who or what shifted this 69-foot-long stone? Giants? At the Gigantia temple on Gozo.

In the epic world of the Greeks, we hear about giants not only in the *Argonautica* but also in the later tale of Odysseus, who did battle with them. These powerfully-built figures are supposed to have been the fruit of a sexual union between men and gods. I have good reasons to believe that these same giants were responsible for the huge megalithic constructions which intrigue archaeologists, such as on the small islands of Malta and Gozo. The mighty ruins of a temple there still bear the name "Gigantia" (see Images 1 and 2).

The Argo continued its journey without any more major upsets, except that a sea-god called Glaucos shot up to the surface suddenly like a submarine from the depths. He brought the Argonauts a message from Zeus, for Heracles and his darling Hylas. Then Glaucos dived quickly under and sank down to the depths. Around him the waves frothed in many spiraling circles and poured over the ship.

In Salmydessos, the Argonauts encountered an old king who stank to high heaven, and was also starving. The poor fellow was called Phineus. He possessed the gift of prophecy, and had clearly divulged too many of the gods' plans. The punishment they meted out to him was of a strange kind: whenever Phineus wanted to eat something, two winged creatures swooped down from the clouds and snatched the food away from him. Whatever they didn't snatch they covered in filth so that it stank and was inedible. When the Argonauts arrived the old man hardly had the strength to move. He asked the Argonauts for help and promised to reward them by warning them of approaching dangers. Not of all dangers, though, for Phineus suspected that this was precisely what the gods didn't want. The Argonauts felt sorry for him and prepared for themselves and the stinking king a luxurious feast. Just as the king was about to eat, the flying creatures—Harpies—swooped down from clear skies upon the food. But this time things turned out differently. Two of the Argonauts had the ability to fly, and pursued the fleeing Harpies into the air. The airborne Argonauts soon returned and told the king he now had nothing more to fear from the Harpies. They had been in hot pursuit behind them and would easily have been able to kill them—but the goddess Iris had commanded that they spare them, for they were the "dogs of Zeus."

Just pure invention and fairy tale, one may be tempted to say. Someone rises up to the surface of the sea and makes the water spin, two Argonauts take off into the air with incredible speed, and Zeus, the father of the gods, possesses flying dogs. But this is only the modest beginning of a baffling science-fiction story from ancient times. Things get much more confusing!

The king, who by now smelled perfectly nice and was finally able to eat in peace, kept his promise and told the Argonauts of a few impending dangers. He described the route to Colchis which now lay before them, and warned particularly of two giant cliff walls which opened and shut like doors and crushed every vessel that did not get through at the right place and the right moment. The old king advised them to take a dove with them, and let it fly before them through the gap in the cliff walls. Apollonius says:

> Now they steered into the foaming Bosphorus sound. The waves rose up like hills, threatening to collapse into the ship, often rising higher than the clouds. No one imagined that they would escape with their lives...but however terrible the waves, they become tame when a clever, experienced pilot has the tiller in his hand....[32]

The word "pilot" is not my invention. It appears in the 1779 translation of Apollonius. The king had described the route to the Argonauts down to the last detail; clearly he knew every bay and mountain, as well as the names of the countries and their rulers. Strangely enough, the king refers twice to the danger of the Amazons:

> Further on you will come to the lands of Doan and the towns of the Amazons.... Do not for a moment think of coming ashore at a deserted place, where you will have trouble driving off the most unashamed birds who swoop around the island in great flocks. It is here that the rulers of the Amazons...have built their god a temple....[33]

The aging ruler even knows all about the Golden Fleece:

> When you pass up-river through the estuary, you will have Aietes' tower before you, and the shady grove of Mars, where the Fleece

is.... It is guarded by a Lindworm, a terrible wonder. Neither day nor night does sleep press down its lids, never does he cease his constant watch....[34]

This lindworm, or dragon, reminds one of a kind of robot with a multitude of sensors. What kind of animal is it which has no bodily needs, never sleeps, and constantly watches everything around it? Similar creatures are described in other ancient texts, such as the *Epic of Gilgamesh*, which was found in the hill of Kujundshik, the former Nineveh. The clay tablets on which it was written came from the library of the Assyrian king Assurpanipal. This epic describes how Gilgamesh and his friend Enkidu climb up the mountain of the gods, on the top of which stood the shining white tower of the goddess Irnini. Just before they reach it, the fearful being Chumbaba approaches them. Chumbaba had paws like a lion, his body was covered in iron scales, his feet were armed with claws, horns shone upon his head, and his tail ended in a snake's mouth. He must have been a frightful monster. The two companions shot arrows at him and threw spears, but all their missiles glanced off. From the mountain of the gods, bolts of lightning flared up: "a fire flamed up, it rained death. The brightness passed, the fire went out. All that had been struck by lightning turned to ash."[35]

A little later Enkidu dies of an incurable illness. Terribly concerned, Gilgamesh asks: "Were you perhaps poisoned by the breath of the sky creature?" Whatever this "sky creature" was, it seems to have caused Enkidu's death. During the further course of the story, "a door speaks like a person"! The speaking beam in the Argo does the same thing. And then there is the "Park of the Gods" that is guarded by two ugly mixed beings, gigantic "scorpion people." Only their chests are visible above the earth, the rest of their bodies being anchored in the ground: "Horrible, frightful they look, and their gaze means death. The dreadful flashing of their eyes makes mountains roll down to the valleys."[36]

Nevertheless, the scorpion people in the *Epic of Gilgamesh* have intelligence, more than can really be said of the lindworm and dragon guardians. Gilgamesh can talk with them, and they warn him of approaching dangers both on land and sea, just as King Phineus did to the Argonauts.

Phineus advises the Argonauts to take Euphemus with them on board. He was the one who let the dove fly between the two cliff walls, and who was also able to speed over water without getting his feet wet.

For 40 days the Argonauts relaxed in Phineus' kingdom. (In the *Epic of Gilgamesh*, it takes 40 hours to reach the "Mountain of Cedars.") A group of Argonauts slept on board the Argo, the others in the king's palace. They restocked their provisions and set up an altar in honor of Jupiter. On the 41st day, the Argo set off down a winding river or canal. The Argonauts soon caught sight of the "swimming islands" with the dangerous cliff walls, and Euphemus sprang into action:

> They steered slowly and with great care. Their ears were already deafened from afar by the crash of the rocks falling shut above. And loudly crashed back the echo of the wave-churning shores. Now Euphemus raised himself to the gable of the ship, holding the dove in his hand.... Yet they were afraid. Euphemus released the dove, they all raised their heads to watch it fly. But the cliff walls crashed together again from both sides, a deafening noise. From the sea great breakers of water sprayed upwards and the air hurtled around and around...the current dragged the ship backwards. The sharp rocks of the cliff just sheared off the dove's outermost feathers, but she herself came through unharmed. The sailors cried aloud for joy...now the rock-walls tore far open again...since an unexpected wave rose up suddenly...when they saw it they were afraid it would swamp their vessel. But Tiphys eased them with a quick turn, so that the wave burst upon the good ship's figure-head, then lifted it right up above the rocks, so that it floated gracefully there in the air.... Now the ship hung there like a hanging beam, but Minerva pressed her left hand against the rock and with her right gave the ship a push. Swift as a feathered arrow it flitted past the cliff.... This was meant to be, it was destiny.[37]

Tiphys, the Argo's steersman, calmed his overwrought companions. Though they had escaped the terrible danger of the cliff walls, this miracle had only been possible with the help of the gods. Minerva had lent a helping hand, and the goddess Athene had given advice during the building of the ship, so that the Argo was "joined together by strong brackets and made unsinkable."[38]

It was clear that the dangers could not have been overcome without divine aid. Now and then the Olympians also showed themselves. Shortly after their adventure with the crashing cliff walls, the Argonauts caught sight of the god Apollo flying over the Argo on his way from Lycia. This happened en route to the land of the Hyperboreans, which lay on the other side of the North Winds. Apollo was visiting "peoples of another race," and the islands echoed to the sound of his flying boat. This once more shook the Argonauts to their core, so that they were moved to build him an altar. Soon after this Tiphys, the experienced pilot of the Argo, fell ill and died. His fellow voyagers raised a pyramid over his grave—astonishing really, as burial pyramids were not supposed to have appeared until the Egypt of the pharaohs.

During the following days, the Argonauts sailed around the "many bays on the cape of the Amazons."[39] A mighty river is described, unlike any other on earth, for a hundred other rivers are said to flow into it. Yet this river flows only from a single source, which comes down from the "Amazonian mountains." The river, it is said, flows backward and forward through many provinces and (in Apollonius' version):

> No one knows for sure how many of its tributaries creep away through the land.... If the noble travellers had stayed longer on its banks, they would have had to do battle with the women, and blood would have been spilled, for the Amazons are swift and pay little heed to justice. They love war above all, and take pleasure in using force. They descend from Mars and Harmonia.[40]

The crew was not that keen on picking a fight with these Amazons, who ran down to the shore in full battle gear the moment they saw the Argo. The Argonauts had not forgotten the old King Phineus' words, warning them of the Amazons. The old man had also spoken of "disaster in the sky," and this followed a few days after they had left the bays of the Amazons.

As they landed on a lonely shore, the Argo was suddenly attacked by birds, which shot sharp and deadly arrows down on the Argonauts. The latter defended themselves by raising their shields over their heads, so forming one big protective barrier the length of the Argo. Other members of the crew began to utter a terrible noise which irritated the birds and sent them flying off.

The Argonauts went ashore. The whole region was dried up and there was no real reason for staying. Yet suddenly there appeared four stark-naked, emaciated figures, suffering from hunger and thirst, who only just had the strength to beg Jason for help. They said they were brothers, had been shipwrecked, and had clung on to bits of wreckage until being washed up on this island the night before. The Argonauts realized that these were the four sons of Prixos, who had once flown to Colchis with his sister on the Golden Fleece. They were a wonderful addition to the Argo's crew, for they knew all about the grove where the Golden Fleece was held, and how to get there. One of the four sons of Prixos was called Argos, and it was he who, in the dead of night, guided the Argo to the Colchis coast, and from there to the mouth of the Phasis River. On its shore lay the town of Aia, with the king's palace and—some way off—the grove where the Golden Fleece was.

What was the best way to proceed? Jason thought they could try the gentle approach first, and talk to the tyrant King Aietes who ruled the land of Colchis. The Argonauts knew that King Aietes was a violent ruler who did not keep his word, but on the other hand they had saved the lives of Prixos' four sons, who were his nephews. The Argonauts built an altar and asked the gods for advice.

Some of the gods—the names are confusing and not important here—asked the young god of love Eros to arrange for the daughter of the tyrant, pretty Medeia, to fall hopelessly in love with Jason. This would lead her to help the Argonauts even against the will of her evil father. The goddess Hera joined in this "divine conspiracy" and shrouded the men who went to visit the palace in a kind of mist. This made the heroes invisible, so that they suddenly stood before the palace without having been noticed by soldiers and guards. The gods also made sure that Medeia would be the first person to catch sight of Jason. At the same moment Eros shot his arrow into the girl's heart, so that she could not stop gazing at him.

What else could King Aietes do but welcome his uninvited guests? After all, they were bringing back his lost nephews, and his own daughter was asking him to arrange a meal with them. Jason tried to be diplomatic. He mentioned the fact that they were all related to each other through the race of gods, and that he had come to ask for the Golden Fleece.

King Aietes no doubt thought he had misheard. He had never for a moment dreamed of even putting the Golden Fleece on display, and now here was this young whippersnapper daring to ask for the greatest treasure of his kingdom. Aietes laughed aloud, and said, cunningly, that Jason could have the Golden Fleece if he passed three tests.

Outside the grove where the Golden Fleece was nailed, said sly Aietes, there were also caves where fire-spitting bulls lived. Jason must harness these bulls to a plough and till the field with them. Then he must sow dragon's teeth in the furrows, which would quickly grow into frightful figures who must be fought and conquered. Jason would also have to deal with the fire-spitting dragon who never slept.

The shifty ruler knew very well that no one could do this. He did not think he was in the remotest danger of losing the Golden Fleece. However, he had reckoned without the "divine conspiracy." After the evening feast Jason and his friends returned rather glumly to the Argo. They too thought the task was beyond them. Jason complained bitterly to his companions about the dreadful king's conditions:

He says he has two untameable bulls on the field of Mars. Their feet are iron, they breathe flames. With these I must plough four acres of land. Then he wants to give me seed from the mouth of a dragon. From them, he says, armoured men will grow, whom I must kill before the day is done.[41]

But Jason's new lover, the king's daughter Medeia, knew how to help. She possessed a strange ointment with unusual effects. This miracle cure came from a medicinal herb that had grown from the blood of Prometheus the Titan. She told Jason to rub it all over his body and on his weapons. The ointment would protect him from heat and fire so that the fire-spitting bulls could not harm him. His weapons would also become invincibly strong, and give him superhuman powers.

Jason passed a quiet night, then washed himself thoroughly, made a sacrifice to the gods, smeared himself and his weapons all over with the miracle ointment, and pulled on his clothes. Soon after began the strangest battle described anywhere in ancient literature:

> Suddenly, from the secret cavern, the locked stall, the whole air was full of acrid smoke. The two bulls shot forth, breathing fire from their nostrils. The heroes were seized with fright when they saw them. But Jason stood firm, his feet steady, and waited for their attack. He held his shield before him as they bellowed and at the same time struck him with their strong horns, but they were unable to move him even an inch from his position. As when the bellows in the blacksmith's stove sets the fire fiercely roaring with a fearful rush and noise of heat, so the bulls blew flames from their mouths and bellowed at the same time. The heat engulfed the hero like a bolt of lightning, but the lady's ointment protected him. And now he seizes the nearest bull by the point of its horns, and draws it by sheer force to the iron yoke. Then he trips up the iron foot with his own foot and floors the beast.[42]

As King Aietes had demanded, Jason ploughed the field with these unruly, fire-spitting animals, then threw the dragon's teeth upon the furrows. Soon dreadful figures sprouted up everywhere on the battlefield, armed with metal spikes and shining helmets, and the soil beneath them shone white hot and lit up the night.

Jason took a mighty lump of stone, so large that even four men couldn't have raised it, and threw it in the midst of the swelling ranks of monsters. They were confused and did not know where the attack was coming from. This gave Jason the chance to wreak havoc:

> From the scabbard he drew the sword and with it stabbed whatever came his way. Many who were up to their navels in the ground

still, and others who were still up to their shoulders. There were others, too, who had just got up on their feet, and then a whole crowd who had run into the battle too soon. They fought and fell.... Thus Jason mows them down...the blood ran in the furrows like streams of spring water...some fell on their faces and got mouthfuls of soil, others on their backs, others on their sides and arms. Of great girth they were, monstrous as whales.[43]

Jason made a clean sweep of them. But the worst was still to come: the dragon who never slept, who guarded the Golden Fleece. Together with his lover, Jason went to the grove where the Golden Fleece was fastened to a beech tree:

So they looked around for the shady beech and the Fleece upon it...it shone like a cloud that is illumined by the setting rays of the sun. But the Lindworm on the tree, who never sleeps, stretched out its long neck. It whistled in a horrible way. The hills and the deep grove rang with the sound...clouds of smoke filled the flaming wood, wave after wave of bright smoke snaked up out of the earth into the upper air, like the monster's lengths of knotty tail, which were covered in hard scales.[44]

Jason could not see how to get around this monster, but once more his lover helped him. She smeared an elder branch with her special ointment and waved it around in front of the dragon's glowing eyes. At the same time she spoke magic words, and the monster grew visibly slower and more soporific, until it finally laid its head upon the ground. Jason climbed the tree and released the Golden Fleece. The strange object glowed red, and was too large for Jason to carry on his shoulders. The ground below the Golden Fleece also shone the whole time that Jason was fleeing with it back to the Argo.

Once back on board, everyone wanted to touch the Golden Fleece, but Jason forbade this and covered it with a great blanket. There was no time for feasting or celebrations. Jason and the king's daughter were afraid that King Aietes would do all in his power to get this unique treasure back. The Argonauts sailed as fast as they could down the river, and out to the open sea.

King Aietes, who had never meant to keep his word, ordered up a great fleet, which he divided so as to come at Jason and the Argonauts from both sides. Aietes' ship reached a country whose inhabitants had never seen such travellers, and who therefore believed them to be sea monsters. (There is a similar story in the Ethiopian "Book of Kings," the *Kebra Negest*, which tells how Baina-lehkem steals the greatest treasure of the time from his father Solomon: the Ark of the Covenant. Solomon sends his warriors to get it back. The chase is pursued—partly by flying machines—from Jerusalem to the [modem-day] town of Axum in Ethiopia.)

After a few minor adventures, which are described differently in various versions of the *Argonautica*, the Argo reached the "amber islands." The talking beam in the prow of the ship warned the crew of the wrath of Zeus. (In the meantime the ship's keel began to talk with audible voice.) The father of the gods was furious, for Jason had managed to kill the brother of his beloved. This did not occur through jealousy, but because Medeia had spun an intrigue. Later on in the story Jason was absolved of this murder, and Zeus was satisfied. On various islands and in many different lands the Argonauts raised altars and memorials. At some point the Argo ran far up into the rivers of Eridian. Astonished, one learns that "This is where Phaethon fell from the sun chariot down into the deepest sea when Jove's flaming thunderbolt half burned him. This sea still stinks of sulphur...no bird spreads its wings and flies over it."[45]

This is a strange reference. The story of Phaethon and his sun chariot is very ancient, and has not been precisely dated. The Roman poet Ovid gives it in full in his Metamorphoses, though Ovid lived about 40 years before Christ, at a time when the *Argonautica* has already existed for centuries. According to this tale, Phaethon was a son of the sun god Helios. One day Phaethon visited his father in the sky and asked him to fulfill one wish, because the earth-dwellers did not believe that he was really related to the sun god. He asked to be allowed to drive the sun chariot. His father was horrified and continually warned his offspring to give up the idea, telling him that to drive the sun chariot required quite particular knowledge. Typically, Phaethon didn't want to heed these warnings. His father had unwittingly promised to fulfill his every wish, and so couldn't get out of it now. The fiery horses were therefore refueled with four-star ambrosia, and harnessed up to the wagon.[46]

The sun chariot raced out into the sky, but the horses soon noticed that their driver couldn't control them. They broke out of their usual course, rose high up into the sky then sped at dizzying speed down toward the earth again. This went on for a while—up, down, and all over the place—until the sun chariot started to get closer and closer to the earth. The clouds started steaming and whole forests and stretches of land caught fire. But the air in the heavenly vehicle also got hotter and hotter so that Phaethon could hardly breathe. As the fire engulfed his hair and skin, there was nothing left for him to do but leap out of the chariot, and his body was said to have fallen into the Eridanos River. His sisters, the Heliades, went there and wept so long that their tears turned to amber, which one still finds on the river's banks. The heavenly chariot crashed with a shower of sparks into a lake.

Nowadays the tale of Phaethon is seen as a double parable. On the one hand is the sun which has the power to burn up whole stretches of land, on the other the young man who thinks that he can do anything his father can. I doubt whether this story was originally regarded by those who told it simply as a parable. Too many of its elements are too logical and show parallels with modern space travel technology. But this is equally true of other parts of the *Argonautica*.

After all, it is not just a matter of course if amphibious vehicles turn up in a tale that is millennia old. Apollonius tells us, "Out of the sea leapt a horse of unusual size, and came ashore. Its mane was golden, its head was high, and it shook off the salty foam from its sides. Then it ran off on feet as swift as the wind."[47]

This amphibious horse is meant to have been one of Poseidon's horses. Poseidon was the god of the sea, but also the god of Atlantis. We'll come to that story later on. So what was going on here? Is Poseidon's horse an isolated episode, something that only the Argonauts saw? Far from it.

In the Bible, in the book of the Prophet Jonah (Chapter 2), we can read the episode in which Jonah survived for three days and nights in the belly of a whale. Theologians say that this is meant prophetically, in reference to the three days from Jesus' death to His resurrection. An absurd ideal. One learns more in Volume III of the book *Die Sagen der Juden* ("Tales of the Jews From Ancient Times"). Here we read that Jonah entered the jaws of the fish just as "a man enters a room." It must have been a strange fish because its eyes were like "windows, and also shone inwards." Of course, Jonah was able to speak with the fish, and through its eyes—portholes!— he could see, "bathed in light, as in the midday sun," all that was happening in the sea and on the ocean floor.[48]

There is a parallel to this prehistoric submarine in the Babylonian Oannes Tale. Around 350 BC, a Babylonian priest wrote three works. He was called Berossus and served his god Marduk (also called Bel or Baal). The first volume of his book, the Babylonic, deals with the creation of the world and the starry firmament, the second volume with the Babylonian kingdom, and the third was a proper history. Berossus' books are only preserved in fragments, but other ancient historians quote from them, such as the Roman Seneca, or Flavius Jospehus, a contemporary of Jesus. And in the 1st century after Christ, Alexander Polyhistor of Milet wrote about the Babylonians. Thus bits and pieces of Berossus' work have survived the millennia.

This Babylonian priest also described a curious being, Oannes, that came out of the Eryteian Sea beside Babylon. This creature, he said, had the shape of a fish, but with a human head, human feet, and a tail, and had spoken like a human being. During the day Oannes had conversed with people, without eating anything. He had taught them not only knowledge of written signs and sciences, but also how to build towns and erect temples, how to introduce laws and measure the land, and everything else they might need to know. Since this time, no one had invented anything which exceeded his teaching. Before departing, Oannes had given the people a book containing his instructions.

Not bad for a teacher from the water. Of course, one can dismiss the Oannes tale as fantasy, as with every incredible story, but Oannes also forms part of the traditional tales of other ancient peoples. The Parsees call the teacher from the water "Yma,"[49] the Phoenicians call it "Taut," and there is even a monster with the body of a horse and the head of a dragon who rises up out of the depths of the ocean at the time of the Chinese emperor Fuk-Hi. This must have been a strange creature indeed, for its body was adorned with written signs.[50]

The amphibious horse in the *Argonautica* also turned out to be a speaking creature. The heroes and their vessel had come to a lake which had no opening to the sea. The team kept going by towing the Argo over land— probably with the help of wooden rollers. Finally they made an offering to the gods of a tripod which Jason was supposed to have received in Delphi, and straight away the amphibious creature reappeared. It was apparently called Eurypylus, another son of Poseidon. Eurypylus first appeared in the form of a beautiful and friendly youth, with whom one could have excellent conversations. He wished the Argonauts good luck on their further travels, showed them which way the sea was, and walked off with the tripod into the cold water. Then he grasped hold of the Argo's keel and pushed the ship off into the current:

> The god took pleasure in the worship afforded him, rose out of the depths and appeared in the shape of body natural to him. As a man will lead a horse into the swiftest course...he took hold of the Argo's keel and led it gently into the sea.... But his lower body was divided into two separate fish tails. He beat the water with the pointed ends, which appeared crescent-shaped like the horns of the moon, and led the Argo until they came to the open sea. Then he suddenly vanished down into the depths. The heroes raised a loud shout when they saw this wonder.[51]

The "shout" of the Argonauts was quite understandable. When earthly forces don't help, super-earthly ones have to. Jason's friends carried on sailing and rowing for home, passing many countries on their way. On the heights of Crete they wanted to replenish their stocks of water, but this was prevented by Talos, who was endowed with an invulnerable, metal body. He is described as a "bronze giant,"[52] or as a being whose "whole body was covered in bronze."[53] According to Apollonius, Talos encircled the island three times in a year, but all other ancient authors speak of "three times a day."[54] With his magic eyes he caught sight of every vessel which approached Crete, then pelted it from a great distance, apparently with rocks, with great accuracy. He also had the ability to radiate heat, drawing boats toward him and letting them go up in flames. Talos was said to have been made by the god Hephaestus, who was a son of Zeus. The Romans worshipped him as the god of fire, and named him Vulcanus. For the Greeks Hephaestus was both god of fire and protector of blacksmiths.

Zeus was said to have given Talos to his former beloved Europa, who once lived with this father of the gods on Crete. The reason they had gone there is shrouded in mythology. The Greeks assumed that Europa was the daughter of King Tyrros. When she was a girl, and playing with her animals, Zeus had come by and fallen for her. Zeus changed himself into a young and handsome bull, and Europa had gently got up on his back. This bull must have been another kind of amphibious machine, for hardly had Europa taken her seat than it plunged into the sea and swam with its lovely cargo to Crete. There, I assume, it turned back into a man, who made love to Europa. But gods are not constant in love; divine business required Zeus to leave Crete, and he gave Talos to his beloved, to guard the island from undesired visitors.

Although Talos was invulnerable, he did have a weak spot. On his ankle was a sinew covered in tanned skin, and under it lay a bronze nail or a golden screw. If this bolt was opened, then colorless—other writers say white or festering—blood poured out, and Talos would be incapacitated.

Jason and his Argonauts tried to approach Crete, but Talos spied the Argo and began to fire upon it. Once more it was Medeia, by now Jason's wife, who suggested rowing out of range. She said that she knew a magic way of putting Talos out of action. Apollonius tells us:

> They would gladly have sailed to Crete, but Talos, the steel man, prevented the noble ones tying up on shore with the dew still on their mast. For he hurled stones at them. Talos was one of the iron race of the earthly ones...a half god, a half man. Jupiter gave him to Europa to defend the island. Three times in each year he circled Crete with feet of iron. Ironclad and invincible was his body, but he

had a vein of blood on the ball of his foot under the ankle, lightly covered by skin. This is where death lurked close to his life.[55]

The Argonauts quickly rowed away from the bombardment and out to the open sea. Medeia began to recite magic spells and to call upon the spirits of the abyss, which, once they have been called up, split the air. Then she cast a spell on Talos' eyes so that imaginary pictures filled his gaze. Irritated, Talos knocked the sensitive place on his ankle against a cliff, and blood flowed out of the wound like molten lead:

> Although he was made of iron, he succumbed to the magic...so he knocked his ankle against a sharp stone, and a sap like molten lead flowed out of him. He could no longer stand upright and fell over, just as a pine tree falls from the summit of a mountain.... Then he picked himself up again and stood upon his huge feet—but not for long for he fell to the ground again with a mighty crash.[56]

Talos tumbled helplessly back and forth, trying to right himself, but then lost his balance altogether and plunged with a horrific noise into the sea.

Now the Argo came to Crete's shores and could anchor safely. But the Argonauts were longing for home by now, and after all they had a trophy to show—the Golden Fleece. After a short sojourn on Crete they headed off again to sea, and suddenly everything around them became dark. No star was visible any longer, and they seemed to be in some sort of underworld. The air was black as pitch—no spark of light, and no glint of moon. Jason begged Apollo not to leave them now, so near to their destination; he promised to offer many gifts in the temples of their homeland. Apollo shot down from the sky and lit up the whole surroundings with bright arrows. In their light the Argonauts caught sight of a small island, close to which they anchored. They set up a holy place in honor of Apollo, and called the islet Anaphe.

The rest of the story is quickly told.

The Argo sailed past several Greek islands and reached the harbor of Pagasai, where their journey had begun, without further problem. Jason and his crew were given a heroes' welcome. Then follow a few family intrigues. Jason is said to have turned his attentions to another young lady, behavior which his wife Medeia frowned upon. She poisoned her children, put a curse on Jason's girlfriend, and the poor fellow threw himself on his sword in desperation. So our divine hero ends the story rather unfittingly with suicide.

And what happened with the Golden Fleece? Below what castle or fortress does the skin of the flying ram lie buried? Who used it? Did it reappear again? In which museum can one admire it? The greatest voyage of ancient times took place because of the Golden Fleece. The thing must have been of enormous value to its new owner. But there is nothing more to be found in ancient literature; the trail of the Golden Fleece disappears in the mists of time.

Many authors and brilliant historians have told tales of the Argonauts, and the historians and exegetes of today have tried to understand the journey of the Argo. Where did the ship go? Where did the adventures take place? On which coasts, on which islands and mountains might one find the many altars and memorials which the Argonauts raised? Apollonius often gives us very precise geographical locations in his *Argonautica*, with many accompanying descriptions. My emphases in the following examples show how detailed Apollonius' account is, and how seriously he takes his geography:

> At Pytho, in the fields of Ortigern...they sailed with the wind behind them past the outermost horn, the Capes Tisae...behind them vanished the dark land of the Pelasges.
>
> From there they sailed to Meliboa, and saw the wild waves breaking upon its rocky coast. And with the new day saw Homola which is built beside the sea. They left it behind them, and also soon passed the river mouth leading from the water of Amyrus. Then they caught sight of the plains of Eurymenas, and the deep folds of Olympus. Also Canastra.... In the twilight of evening, they glimpsed the peak of Mount Atho, whose shadow covers the island of Lemnos.

Until they came once more to the coasts of the Dolions...where they saw the Macriades rocks, and in front of them the land of Thrace. Also the airy mouth of the Bosphorus, the hill of Mysen, and in the other direction the Aesaps and Nepeia River.

To the welcome mouth of the Calichor river. It was here that Bacchus once celebrated his orgies, when the hero returned to Thebes from the peoples of India.

Then they came to the land of Assyria...the early rays of dawn caressed the snowy peaks of the Caucasus.

In those days the Deucalides ruled the land of the Pelasges. But Egypt, the mother of the oldest race of men, was already growing in notoriety and fame...

They sailed further and dawn found them in the Land of the Hyllers. A large number of islands lay before them, and it is dangerous for ships to pass through them.

Iris descended from Olympus, ploughing through the air with outstretched wings, and alighting at the Aegean Sea.

Here rose Scylla from the waters...there roared Charybdis.[57]

These are only a few examples, which show that Apollonius knew very well in what part of the world the heroes of the Argo were conducting their adventures. Not only rivers, islands or specific regions are mentioned, but also seas or mountain ranges like the Caucasus. Ought it not to be very easy to plot the Argonauts' journey?

Of course, this has been done—with very variable results. The two French professors Emile Delage and Francis Vian drew up clear maps,[58, 59] according to which Jason and his crew journeyed from the Caucasus at the eastern end of the Black Sea along the river Istros (the Danube) to the Adriatic, passing other tributaries on their way. In the Fo valley there were many small and larger rivers, which the Argonauts somehow managed to use to sail round the Alps, and to reach the Rhine and the Rhône. In the region of present-day Marseilles they arrived at the Mediterranean again, and passed through the straits of Messina—the supposed Scylla and Charybdis. Finally they turned east in the direction of the (present) Ionian islands, then turned south and headed straight for the Great Syrtis of Libya. From there they sailed home via Crete. And where is the place where Phaethoe's heavenly chariot crashed to earth? Not far from the western edge of Switzerland, in the Marais de Pháyton (Marsh of Phaethon)!

Reinhold and Stephanie Glei[60, 61] provided still more exact maps. But I have problems with these; how does one get from the river Istros or Danube to the Adriatic, and from there via the Eridanos River in the Po valley to the "Celtic seas" of present-day France? After all, the Argo was not some rubber dinghy, but the greatest vessel of the age, with a crew of 50. It cannot be denied that there may have been waterways in those days which no longer exist—which would once more throw up the question of the date of the original *Argonautica*. At which geological epochs did navigable waterways exist where now there is only dry land?

A consul general of France, Monsieur R. Roux, compares the wanderings of Odysseus, described in great detail by the Greek poet Homer, with the *Argonautica*: "One must never forget the great precision and differentiation of Strabo: the Odyssey takes place in the western ocean, the Argosy in the eastern."[62]

Christine Pellech has a quite different view. Her very thorough study also compares Odysseus' wanderings with the *Argonautica*, concluding that "the Odyssey partly overlaps with the journey of the Argonauts." She says that Odysseus actually sailed right round the world—millennia before Columbus—and puts forward the view that the Egyptians had drawn on Phoenician sources, and it was this "Phoenician-Egyptian mixture that was taken over wholesale by the Greeks." The content of both the *Argonautica* and the Odyssey derives from Egypt, according to Pellech, and she substantiates this by the fact that Apollonius of Rhodes grew up in Alexandria, visited the library there, and only left Egypt after falling out with his teacher.[63]

Christine Pellech's arguments read like well-documented research, and she also succeeds in identifying many points on the journey with actual places on the globe. Many questions still remain, however.

If what she says is true, then most of the geographical indications given by Apollonius must be wrong, and many scholars would have been wasting their time. What could the explanation be? Let us assume that Apollonius really brought the core of the Argonaut story from Egypt to Greece. Then, to conjure up a fuller picture for himself, he might well have adorned it with geographical details from his own experience. To do this, though, he would have to have had an extensive knowledge of the wide realms of the Greek world in those days, and also many rivers, coasts, and mountains beyond Greece. But even then we are left with difficulties; how, for instance, can one explain passages by Apollonius such as the following:

> In the evening they came ashore on the Atlantides Island. Orpheus begged them not to spurn the solemnities of the island, nor the secrets, the laws, customs, the religious rites and works. If they observed these they would be assured of the love of heaven on their further voyage over the dangerous ocean. But to speak further of these things I do not dare.[64]

Let's not forget that Atlantis was the island of the god Poseidon, that two of Poseidon's sons were said to have travelled on the Argo, and that the amphibious vehicles which had surfaced from the sea had been the work of Poseidon. But how does Apollonius know about Atlantis—if that is what the word "Atlantides" refers to? He writes at least of solemnities which one should not spurn, but also of secrets, laws, and customs. And, though everywhere else he gives each little geographic detail, he now refrains from saying anything further about such things. Something doesn't quite fit here, and I will return to the Atlantis story later.

Did the Argo journey ever actually take place? As long as we have no older sources to draw on than the ones cited here, we will probably never know. But I have been chasing the trail of the gods for the past 40 years, convinced that many elements of the *Argonautica* cannot have simply been invented. Imagination is a fine thing, and even millennia ago people enjoyed their flights of fancy. But fantasy is always based on something; it takes its starting point from events which once occurred, from circumstances which cannot be understood, from riddles which our reason cannot neatly pigeon-hole. Nowadays we try hard to put a psychological slant on the "imagination" of the ancients, using the old, worn-out schema of natural phenomena such as lightning and thunder, stars, silence and infinity, volcanic eruptions and earthquakes. But as the history of exegesis or commentary demonstrates, every scholar just thinks in terms of his own experience, conditioned by the time in which he lives. Our so-called "zeitgeist" narrows our perspective and dictates what is "reasonable" or "scientific." My diligent secretary hauled 92 books on the *Argonautica* theme from Bern University library to my study. As usual, one nearly drowns in the miles of commentary written by high-powered academics at different periods—but no one really knows the truth. And every one puts forward a different argument.

I still stand by my basic conviction—on which I have elaborated in 32 books since 1968. All that I try to do is relate new arguments to my original theory, in the process of which the gaps in the mosaic get smaller and smaller, and the overall picture becomes increasingly more convincing. However, I admit that my theory has its blemishes, and that some of what I propose could be explained differently. But at the end of the day, what is the truth? Are the analyses by commentators in the past 100 years correct? Their conclusions convincing? Do they provide—as the scientific community simply assumes—a proven body of knowledge? Or is what they view as scientifically sound just an interpretation dictated by contemporary perspectives?

Here of course I lay myself right open to attack. What, people will say, is Erich von Däniken doing other than interpreting things from his contemporary perspective? That is true. But shouldn't we have learned by now that we are only one living speck of dust in the depths of the universe? That the world and the cosmos are far more fantastic than our school learning tells us. Isn't it time that, given the wealth of material, we admit that something is not quite right with our view of the early history of mankind? And that received views are wrong because they sweep thousands of pointers and hints under the carpet, and refuse even to contemplate them? I do have one advantage over the commentators: I know their arguments, but they don't (care to) know mine.

New readers need to hear my old theories briefly. Sometime or other, many millennia ago, an alien crew landed upon earth. Our forefathers didn't have a clue what was going on; they didn't know anything about technology, let alone space travel. Their simple minds must have regarded the aliens as "gods"—although we all know that there aren't any gods. The aliens first studied small groups and tribes of human beings, just as ethnologists do today. Here and there they gave advice for creating an ordered civilization. There was no language problem between people and "gods," both because our civilization has always managed to pick up totally foreign languages, and because the first *Homo sapiens sapiens* probably learned their language from the "gods" in the first place.

Finally a rift and even mutiny occurred amongst the aliens. They broke the laws of their world of origin and their space commanders, and had sex with pretty daughters of men. Mutants resulted from these unions: huge monsters, the Titans of olden times. Another group of ETs undertook genetic engineering, and created mutants of all kinds. It must have been a real Frankenstein horror scenario. Then the mother spaceship departed with the "good" aliens, back into the depths of the cosmos—though not without having first promised to return at some point in the future.

The "gods" remaining behind on the earth squabbled amongst themselves. They still had bits and pieces of their original technology, and doubtless retained their original knowledge. They knew, for instance, how to work iron, make alloys, create dreadful weapons or robots. But they also knew how to make a hot-air balloon fly, or charge up a sun-powered battery. These "gods" produced children and naturally taught their offspring some of their technological knowledge.

These offspring spread over the earth, inhabiting different regions, which were ruled over in each case either by a single ruler or a family dynasty. They misused their subjects, the human beings, as work-horses, as food-producers, as serviceable idiots. But they also taught them a good deal, and set up the best of them as administrators, so-called kings.

The "gods" basically watched their subjects jealously: "Thou shalt have no other gods before me" was one of their laws. And when it came to battles and blows, the "gods" often supported their subjects with terrible weapons. The sons of the gods and their descendants from third and fourth generations often did battle with another.

So that is my theory, which I backed up from so many sources that the cross references alone turned into a whole book,[65] and all my books together grew not only into an encyclopedia,[66] but also into a CD-ROM. [67, 68] Not to mention the hundreds of books which other authors across the globe have published on the same theme. It is therefore quite natural that I am familiar with all the counter-arguments imaginable, and that I have long since dealt with them to my satisfaction.

What can the *Argonautica* have to do with extraterrestrials? What are the constituent elements which can hardly have just leapt out of the imagination of a group of people who lived X millennia ago? And let me be quite clear on this point: we're not talking about the imagination of some Apollonius, or any other Greek poet, who wrote down their accounts 2,500 years ago. No, the core of the *Argonautica* story comes from a time about which we have no historical records—and this is simply because all the really ancient libraries were destroyed. Unless, of course, some unexpected treasure chamber is about to be opened in Egypt.

So what is it about the *Argonautica* which makes us sit up and take notice?

1. Quite a few of the voyagers are offspring of the gods, from the third and fourth generation. They possess superhuman characteristics.

2. "Mixed beings" are described, such as centaurs, giants with six arms, or the "winged dogs" of Zeus.

3. A goddess makes the Argo unsinkable.

4. The same goddess furnishes the ship with a "speaking beam." This talkative piece of wood must have some hotline to someone, for it warns of approaching dangers.

5. A being called Glaucus surfaces from the waves like a submarine, and brings a message from one of the gods.

6. Cliff walls open and shut as in the tale of Ali Baba and the 40 thieves ("open sesame").

7. King Phineus knows all about the dangers which will be encountered along the route. How?

8. Aietes' tower near the town of Aia.

9. A god (Apollo) flies with noise and commotion over the ship. He is on the way to the land of the "Hyperboreans," and visits "people of another race."

10. Birds shoot deadly arrows, but are irritated by noise.

11. A goddess uses "mist" to make the men invisible.

12. An ointment gives superhuman powers and creates a heat-resistant shield.

13. A dragon which never sleeps, observes everything, has no physical needs, can spit fire, and never dies.

14. Fire-spitting bulls with metal legs.

15. A vehicle of the gods, which needs great experience to drive and control. As it crashes it sets fire to whole stretches of land, and the "pilot" must get out because of the unbearable heat inside it.

16. Various talking amphibious beings.

17. A god who lights up the night by means of "arrows of light."

18. A metallic robot who circles an island. His eyes see ships coming, and he hurls missiles, bums up assailants, and has blood like molten lead.

19. A woman from the race of gods who manages to confuse this robot with "dream images."

Even if we assume that the whole thing is just a tall tale engendered in the head of a dreamer, and later expanded and added to by poets of each succeeding age, does this mean that all questions must fall silent? Is there then no mystery to solve?

Even a tall tale has content. Its original inventor would have had to tell at least a halfway feasible story, for things have to have some cohesion and sense. The basic framework of the story is simple: One or several people set off to seek a unique and extremely valuable object. This object is guarded by an incomprehensible monster, and this all has something to do with the gods.

It doesn't matter much whether the poet also puts in a love story somewhere, which ends happily. But where does the metal monster come from, which attacks ships, shoots things down, radiates heat, and had lead for blood? And where on earth did they get the idea of the fire-spitting dragon? Such creatures never existed in the whole evolution of this planet. No one could have just dreamed it up. There are therefore neither "archetypal" explanations, nor any dim, ancient "memories" at work here. And why does this race of dragons appear time and again in the tales of ancient peoples? The oldest Chinese stories tell of the dragon kings who descended from heaven to earth at the dawn of time. These are no products of fantasy or silly tales, for the dragon kings founded the first Chinese dynasty. No human weapon was able to harm them, and with their fire-spitting dragons they ruled the skies. The dragon kings' flying machines made a terrible noise, and the founder of the first dynasty bore the name "Son of the Red Dragon."[69]

None of this is mythology for, after all, the motif of the fire-spitting dragon influenced all of Chinese art for thousands of years, right up to our own times. And whoever still complains that such things cannot have been true, and that the dragon must be understood in psychological terms, should perhaps take a trip to Beijing and take a look at the great Red Square. What can be seen all along one side of it? The temple of the heavenly emperor!

Doesn't it gradually occur to you that something is odd here? That all the accounts from antiquity are not just legends, myths, or imaginary fairy-tales, but a former reality? This far-off reality, however, can be proven in another way too: by following the trail of time itself.

Chapter 2
In the Name of Zeus

*The Ten Commandments are so clear and definite because
they weren't decided by conference.*

—Konrad Adenauer, 1876–1967

The region which we call Olympia was already inhabited in the 3rd millennium BC. The first holy place in that part of western Peloponnesia was dedicated to the goddess Ge. Much later, Olympia developed into the temple city of Zeus. In the year 776 BC, the first competitions were held at Olympia, and we have a written record of the name of the victor— "Coroibos from Elis." Athletic competitions took place here every four years, over a total span of 1,168 years, from 776 BC to AD 393. Strict rules were drawn up, both for the competitors and the audience. The athletes had to have trained for at least 10 months; they also had to be free Greeks, who had not committed a murder nor behaved indecently in a holy place. Thirty days before the games began, the athletes gathered in the training camp at Elis, 35 miles (57km) from Olympia, where they lived together in simple dwellings, all receiving the same food.

The Olympic Games were only for the men; women and slaves were not even allowed to watch, and there was a law which actually said that any woman caught watching the games would be thrown off Mount Typaion. Why were they so against women? All participants had to compete naked, and later on the organizers made them train without clothes on as well. Why, for heavens sake? Both the competition judges and the public had to be quite sure that participating athletes were normal human beings, that there was no cheating, and that everyone had the same chance. The word "athlete" actually comes from the Greek word *athlos*, and means prize or honor. And what has all of this to do with the story of the *Argonautica*? Bear with me a little longer.

Up until the 13th Olympic Games in 728 BC, only one single competition took place: the sprint over a stade, a distance of about 200m. Not until 720 BC was a longer run added, over a distance of two stades, about 400m. The first Olympic winner of this race was Acanthos from Sparta. From one Olympic Games to the next after that, new sports were allowed. The history of the games has been researched in detail by various historians. Herodotus, the "father of historians" (490–426 BC), read in person from his works at Olympia, which is how he first became known to his countrymen. The Greek historian Diodorus (about 100 BC), who was the author of 40 volumes of history books, visited the 180th Olympic Games.

Image 3: Megalithic stones at Olympia.

Image 4: Megalithic stones at Olympia.

Image 5: Megalithic stones at Olympia.

It is easy for me to use the history of the Olympic Games to demonstrate that no monsters, giants, Titans, "mixed beings," or other freaks took part. The competitors were naked, and no cross-breed or hermaphrodite would even have been allowed to watch. No robots à la Talos were set to protect the Olympian temples, of which there were a good number, containing gold and silver. No fire-spitting dragons guarded valuable offerings to the gods with tireless eyes, and no "divine" offspring corrupted the games. At least we can be sure of this as far back as 776 BC. Competitions were held in Olympia prior to that, but these were not included in any historical records.

The oldest known reference to the *Argonautica* comes from the IVth poem by Pindar, who scribbled the story down about 500 BC. There were certainly no giants, Titans, or other descendants of the gods around in his day, or they would have been mentioned in the historical records of Olympia. Nor were there any a quarter of a millennium before that, at the first Olympic Games. Nevertheless, the story mentions gods, robots, the Golden Fleece, and an unsleeping dragon. Therefore the first people who told the *Argonautica* story must either have made up their monsters or taken them from far older sources. I can see no alternative.

The fairy-tale invention of a "speaking beam" or a "metal man" does not fit easily in the time of Pindar or even Apollonius. Nor does the unsleeping dragon which has no physical needs, spits fire, and does not die. If such figures were dreamed up in the fairy-tales of the times, we would know about it. In ancient Greece, after all, there was no end of poets and dreamers. Countless numbers of their stories have lasted the millennia, but no single one of them casts scorn on the invented lies of the others. So, surely, these stories must be older than the first Olympic Games.

The deeper we delve into the mists of human history, the more improbable becomes the technical gadgetry, such as that mentioned in the *Argonautica*. Our evolutionary model would lead us to conclude that the further back we go the simpler human thinking would be. Or is there anyone who seriously wants to put forward the view that the fairy-tale tellers reached for their clay tablets the moment that the first writing was invented?

Come with me on a voyage of the mind, which takes us back 4,000 years. We are in the town of Assur, which existed about 2,000 years BC. The development of writing is in full flow, and people are already trying to scratch into clay tablets some laws laid down by their clever ruler. The ruler demands that every one of his subordinates should implement the laws immediately, rather than judge things according to the whim of the moment. Making these "law tablets" is very hard work. First of all, the right mixture of clay must be pressed into square wooden frames, kneaded, and smoothed. Then the scribe draws fine lines in the clay with a sharpened stone. The whole process has been tested for weeks already, by inscribing the soft medium again and again with the wedge-shaped signs. Sometimes the stone tool scratches too deep and the wedge is then too broad at the top, at other times too much pressure is applied. Or the scribe's hand trembles. Often the soft clay sinks just at the wrong place, hiding an important stroke which made one word into its opposite—such as "unjust" out of "just." At last the wooden frames are laid out to dry in the sun. After a few hours one can see that the writing no longer looks right because the heat warps the frame. And many of the tablets break as they are removed from their frames.

You can see, therefore, that writing was both an exhausting process and a grave responsibility 2,000 years BC. Only a few mastered this new art. And now imagine that a dreamer turns up who only has one thing in mind: he demands 5,000 clay tablets in order to inscribe them with a made-up story, a dream, say—or, as one would call it millennia later, a fairy tale! The priests, the tribe, the ruler will only allow such a thing if they regard it as extremely important. And what sort of story would be important enough to spend years engraving it in clay?

Only one, certainly, which tells of an ancient, powerful, and, of course, true series of events, which must be retained for posterity. Lies and inventions are not inscribed in clay—and definitely not dreams.

And this is what happened. After mankind had finally invented writing, or rather had learned it from the gods, what was written down were commercial agreements and later royal decrees or reports of wars and battles. The few, hand-picked experts who were capable of writing did not use this power to record rubbish. The clay tablets were not there to immortalize any dreamer's fantasy. The only things written down were those which were of truly outstanding importance—including tales about the gods, their superhuman weapons and supernatural power. Such tales already existed and were not suddenly invented. There was no place for trivial or escapist literature in the holy texts. Not only the rulers but also the priests would have absolutely refused to countenance that.

So why are descriptions of a mysterious technology of the gods to be found amongst the oldest written records? What made these things so important that they were written down at all? The *Epic of Gilgamesh* was written thousands of years BC, as were the stories of the first Chinese emperors and their heavenly dragons. And in the most ancient version of the Gilgamesh story, written on clay tablets 5,000 or 6,000 years ago, we find the robot Chumbaba, the "tower of the gods," the "door that speaks like a person" and the lightning-rapid missiles of the gods. We also hear of a space journey of course, for Gilgamesh is carried up away from the earth, and describes the view from a great height.

I'd better stop there; I have already explored these tales in other books, to which those who would like to look further can refer.[1, 2]

The historian Dr. Ernst Curtius wrote 190 years ago: "History does not know about the infancy of any race."[3] This is true, for each people only enters historical record after it has formed a community about which something can be written. Herodotus was certainly not the first historian on the planet, history was written down centuries and millennia before him. Herodotus was a scholarly person. He did a thorough job in the libraries of his time, for he was always curious and interested in knowing more, and wanted to find out the real truth about his Greek gods.

Through his diligent research he discovered the origin of the Greek gods in Egypt. He found out that the Egyptians were the first people to keep precise records about their gods and kings, and that they knew of very ancient festivals which "have only recently begun to be celebrated in Greece."[4]

Herodotus discovers his Greek gods, together with all the rites dedicated to them, in ancient Egypt, and he has no compunction in being open about it, although his devout compatriots could easily take offense. Isis, Herodotus declares quite matter-of-factly, is none other than the Egyptian name for Demeter. The goddess Athene and the gods Helios, Ares, and many others all have their origin in Egypt. In the second book of his Histories, from Chapter 60 onward, Herodotus describes diverse festivals honoring these gods, and how they took place in Egypt. He always retains a critical perspective, distinguishing between personal experiences and things which have only been told him at second hand. He also meticulously notes things he does not wish to write about, either because they are sexually offensive, or because he does not believe what he has been told. Herodotus even pursues the question as to why these superhuman beings are called "gods" at all. The answer he comes up with leaves no room for doubt: because they were the original teachers of mankind, and also because "they ordered everything and shared out everything amongst themselves."[5]

Herodotus also derives from his Egyptian sources year-counts which can make us blink in surprise. In Chapter 43 of his second book, he writes that Heracles was known to the Egyptians as a very ancient god. From Heracles to the reign of Amasis, he says, 17,000 years passed. And then he gives two numbers which make the heads of our scholars spin. To the travelling Herodotus—and all this of course happened about 450 BC—the Theban priests read out the names of 341 generations of rulers, which they had carefully recorded. These 341 generations correspond, according to Herodotus, to 11,340 years, and since then there have been "no further gods in human form" in Egypt. Herodotus was not just chatting with simple stonemasons or gossiping traders. The people he was talking to were educated priests; and when, astonished, he asked them if this was true, this elite of priests confirmed that the 341 kings had been people "quite different from the gods," and that before them gods had ruled in Egypt, and lived among human beings. (Whoever wants to check this out can read book 2, Chapters 142 to 145 of Herodotus' *Histories*.) And once more Herodotus assures us that the Egyptians knew "for certain, because they continually reckon the years and record them."[6] The same priests also read to Herodotus from a book the names of all 330 kings, together with the dates of their reign, which followed the reign of Pharaoh Menes.

Our sharp-witted exegetes, philologists, archaeologists, and religious historians of the present day cannot begin to come to terms with these enormous periods of time. Before written history begins, they know only the great black hole of the Stone Age, during which the human beings who had descended from apes slowly and surely expanded their knowledge. They learned to use stone tools and gradually developed a language. They formed closed tribes for safety, invented the arrowhead, the spear, and finally the bow, and at some point found out how to win iron from rock. At the same time, they put up gigantic megalithic constructions. And when they eventually invented writing, they immediately used stone styluses to imprint clay tablets with fairy tales that had a technological slant!

And our experts, who straitjacket their brains in endless conferences and discussions, and who quote from each other's works all the time so as to "remain scientific," cannot come up with any better explanation than the psychological one. They write sentences such as: "To place the chronology of the oldest dynasties before the middle of the 4th millennium is ridiculous and clearly invented."[7] Or: "Complete nonsense," or: "We can happily leave this passage out, for it contains nothing but fantastic nonsense." This kind of viewpoint is absolutely sure that "the history of ancient Egypt only really began around 3000 BC."[8] Any other version of mankind's history is unthinkable, even if the chroniclers of the most varied peoples provide concrete dates. The holy dogma of evolution allows no other alternative.

In order to explain all the inconsistencies, people invent "moon years," accuse the historians and chroniclers of making mistakes with their figures or exaggerating the grandiose nature of their kings, or think up types of calendar which actually never existed—such as the Sothis or Sirius calendar for the Pharaoh kingdoms. And what becomes of our much-praised "scientific approach" if we simply ignore all the dates which so many scribes and chroniclers so carefully recorded? Herodotus is far from being the only one to include dates and periods in his stories. In my last book[9] I showed comparative figures from all over the place. The conclusion to be drawn is not that the ancients had a problem counting, but that we simply don't want to acknowledge the reality of those times.

The Greek philosophers Plato (427–347 BC) and Socrates (470–399 BC) are still regarded, even by our highly advanced culture, as outstanding, sharp-witted thinkers. Their treatises and dialogues fill thousands of pages, and they were always at pains to get at the truth. Whoever reads Plato's *Dialogues* will find out the real meaning of philosophy and dialectics. In his dialogue entitled *The Laws,* Plato enters into conversation with a guest of his from Athens, with Cleinas from Crete and with the Lacedernonian Megillos. These men also discuss past ages, and the Athenian says:

> If we look closer we will find that the paintings and sculptures cre-
> ated 10,000 years ago—and I mean this amount of time precisely,
> not in the usual vague sense of the term—are neither more beauti-
> ful nor uglier.[10]

Why does the Greek emphasize the fact that he means a precise period of "10,000 years"? Because the Greeks regarded all numbers above 10,000 as anything from "big" to "infinite." In Book 3 of the same Dialogue, the men speak quite openly about the downfall of earlier cultures. It is clear that knowledge of these extinct civilizations was self-evident in those days—and not just of small nations decimated at some point or other by war or natural disaster. No, people knew about a global catastrophe caused by a great flood. In Plato, one can read in detail about the eradication of whole countries and cities, and that only small groups survived in mountainous regions. These survivors, he says, had preserved the art of pottery, had lived by hunting, and could make blankets and simple weapons, for they could do this without iron. The use of metals, on the other hand, he says, was taught them by the gods, "so that the human race, in the midst of the travail in which it found itself, would regain fresh impetus and strength to develop."[11]

One can read how the cities of the plains and by the sea were destroyed and all the metal mines were submerged so that it was no longer possible to get new ore. All tools were lost as well, and much knowledge, including the "art of politics." Subsequent generations, says Plato, soon forgot how many millennia had passed. Many people interpret this Dialogue as a kind of assumption, as if Plato were saying "Let's assume this happened, that the world went under and people had to start again from the beginning, how would it be." But this view doesn't have much mileage, for the mention of extinct cultures in Plato is not confined to The Laws. And the Athenian expressly says that he is talking of a precise figure of "10,000 years."

But why should such a catastrophe have occurred? In Plato's Politics one reads with astonishment about: "The miracle of reversal of the rising and setting of the sun and the other heavenly bodies. Where they now rise, there they once set, and rose on the other side."[12] That sounds quite absurd, but in our time gains another dimension. Just imagine a globe and give it a spin around its own axis to get our days and nights. Now tilt the axis over and let the globe continue the same rotation as before—not, in other words, stopping its spin and reversing it. What happens? To the inhabitants of the earth it seems that the sun has changed its path. Of course it hasn't really, but turning the earth's axis in another direction makes it seem so. And a change in the earth's axis will also inevitably lead to terrible floods. Ever since we have known that the magnetic field of our planet shifts, a change in the angle of the earth's axis has been within the bounds of possibility.

Centuries before Plato, the poet Hesiod lived in Greece. Several epics, poems, and fragments of his have survived the millennia. The best known work is his *Theogony*, which was written between 650 and 750 BC.[13] In it he mentions frightful beings who once inhabited the earth. The gods themselves had created them: dreadful figures "with 50 heads, and from their shoulders hung down enormous limbs."[14] The fire-spitting dragon is also already part of Hesiod's menagerie. Apollonius, living 300 years later, cannot therefore have been the inventor of the dragon in the *Argonautica*.

> From the shoulders of the gruesome, snaking dragon grew a hundred heads, its dark tongues flickering and licking about in all directions. From each pair of eyes of the hundred heads light flashes and bums...when he looks his gaze burns like fire. And each of the appalling heads has its own reverberating voice, a wondrous multiplicity of sound.[15]

One can also read in Hesiod's *Theogony* how the goddess Chimaera, from whom we get the word "chimaera" or "mixed being," gave birth to a fire-snorting monster. The monster possessed three heads, that of a lion, a goat and a dragon. The dragon head "snorted the terrible ardour of a fiercely glowing fire."[16]

Once again it is not clear where Hesiod got his information. It is assumed that he too used original Egyptian sources. His accounts are too colorful, too precise and too technologically slanted to have arisen in his own time. In his book *Works and Days,* he writes that the gods created four races before they created the human race: "First the gods, they who dwell on the heights of Olympus, brought forth a golden race of much-discoursing men."[17]

The above quote is translated from a German version of 1817. Professor Voss translated the Greek to read "they who dwell on the heights of Olympus". In newer versions of the same passage, we find a slightly different slant: "[gods] dwelling in heavenly houses."[18]

Let me put these two translations, separated by only 150 years, alongside each other so that you can compare them and draw your conclusions:

1817	1970
"First the gods, they who dwell on the heights of Olympus, brought forth a golden race of much-discoursing men. These were ruled by Chronos, at that time reigning in heaven. And they lived like the gods, their souls continually cared for..."	"Deathless gods dwelling in heavenly houses first created the golden race of frail human beings. That was at the time of Chronos, when he was still king in the heavens. And they lived like gods, having no worry in their hearts..."

The ancient Greek some of us may have toiled over at school is not sufficient to judge which version is more accurate. Although the general drift of both translations is broadly the same, there is a fundamental difference between "heights of Olympus" and "heavenly houses," and between "ruled by Chronos" and "at the time of Chronos." What will the translation sound like in the year 2100? And what was the original sense and meaning in

Hesiod's time? After the "golden race" the gods created a second, lesser race, a "silver race." This race was still created by the same gods, those who "dwell in the heights of Olympus," or, perhaps, "dwell in heavenly houses." This "silver race" was of a lower order than the golden race, both in form and outlook, and was made up of "softies," whose mothers pampered them.

After this came "a third race of noisy people." These were of "great strength and force," and "from their shoulders grew huge limbs."[19] This race is supposed to have been obdurate and obstinate, and its agricultural tools were made of metal. But this race too was a disappointment apparently, and so Chronos created a fourth as well: that of the heroes or half-gods.

We modern people, according to Hesiod, belong to the fifth race, the iron race. We are a mixture of "good and evil," and experience joy and pain. But when things degenerate to such an extent that children no longer resemble their fathers, hosts no longer welcome their guests, and brothers no longer love one another, then our race too will be destroyed in the name of Zeus.

Hesiod gives a vivid, detailed description, including all the finer points of the weapons involved, of the battle between the gods and the Titans. Although the latter had been created by the gods themselves, they had to vanish from the face of the earth. A terrible struggle broke out, in which even father god Zeus got involved, hurling from the skies great exploding bolts of lightning, missiles which made the seas boil, burned whole regions, and brought the earth to its trembling knees. Hesiod uses many pages to describe the slaughter, but I will quote only a short excerpt from the 1817 translation:

> Up above too, the Titans consolidated their squadrons...loudly did the earth quake, and the dome of heaven boomed...and straight from heaven and from Olympus rushed in the Thunderer, with a flash of lightning. Blow fell upon blow, with rumbling and flashing of fire...holy flames intertwined...the fertile sprouting earth flamed up and the great forests collapsed in the fury of fire...then the holy winds caught fire too, so that the eyes of even the strongest were

blinded...as if the domed heaven descended close to the earth, the loudest, most thunderous noise vented itself...the gods stormed in to the fray, the winds blew wildly and whirled up dust and destruction...then Zeus sent his sublime missile...and awful clamour arose...[20]

Such a battle was not waged with earthly means. Something very similar, but with even more dreadful weapons, is described in the Indian epic *The Mahabharata.* There, too, different races of gods do battle with each other:

The unknown weapon is radiant lightning, a frightful messenger of death, which turns to ashes all who belong to the Vrishni and the Andhaka. The bodies consumed by fire were unrecognizable. Those who escaped with their lives lost their hair and their nails. Clay pots broke without cause, the birds turned white. In a short while food became poisonous. The lightning fell to earth and became fine dust.[21]

And what did Gilgamesh say when his friend Enkidu died in great pain after encountering the divine monster Chumbaba? "Was it perhaps the poisonous breath of the heavenly beast which struck you?"[22]

The *Mahabharata* versions available in German are all edited and shortened. Because I can't read Sanskrit, I have to refer mainly to the many volume versions in English. The similarities with Hesiod are too compelling to be simply overlooked.

It was as if the elements had been set free. The sun turned in circles, and burning from the weapon's heat, the world staggered in flames. Elephants were singed by fire and ran wildly to and fro...the water grew hot, the beasts died...the thundering of the flames made the trees crash one after the other as in a forest fire.... Horses and chariots burst into flames...thousands of chariots were destroyed, then a deep silence fell...a terrible sight met the gaze. The corpses of the fallen were disfigured by the awful heat...never before have we seen such a dreadful weapon, never before have we heard of such a weapon.[23]

This is also the place to mention another cross-reference to Gilgamesh: "The heavens cried out, the earth screamed out in reply. Lightning lit up, a fire flamed upwards, death rained down. The brightness vanished, the fire was extinguished. All that had been struck by the lightning turned to ashes."[24]

All these weapons of mass destruction—whether described by Hesiod, or in *The Mahabharata*, or the *Epic of Gilgamesh*—were used in times before written history began. If these battles of the gods had occurred in an "historical epoch," we would have precise accounts with dates. Since this is clearly not the case, they must either have taken place in prehistoric times—or in the imagination. I do understand the point of view of scholars who made their commentaries on these ancient writings before 1945. But since the end of the Second World War, since Hiroshima and Nagasaki, we ought to be a bit wiser. We now know what "gods" are capable of.

The 24,000 couplets of *The Ramayana* are also a treasure trove for the gods' prehistoric activities and technological capabilities. Although the written version of The Ramayana dates back to the 4th or 3rd century BC, the content comes from unknown sources. The hero of the story is the king's son Rama, whose wife Sita is stolen away by the demonic giant Ravana and taken to the island of Lanka—reminiscent of the cause of the Trojan War. With the help of the king of the monkeys (and much technological back-up), Rama succeeds in winning back his wife.[25]

A marvelous vehicle which rises into the air is described in full detail. It resembled a flying pyramid and took off vertically. It was as tall as a three-story building and flew from Lanka (Sri Lanka or Ceylon) to India. The flying machine therefore covered more than 2,000 miles (3,200km). Inside this flying pyramid there was room for several passengers, and also some secret chambers. As it rose up from the ground carrying Rama and Sita, there was a terrible noise. There is a description of how the machine makes the mountains quiver and shake, and heads off upward with the sound of thunder, but also sets fire to buildings, fields, and forests. Decades before Hiroshima, in 1893, Professor Hermann Jacobi commented: "There is no doubt whatsoever that this must refer simply to a tropical storm."[26]

As I said before, after Hiroshima we should be a little wiser. But the commentaries which experts still make about these ancient texts make me feel as though we're stuck in the wrong age. To me, it is clear that much of what the ancient chroniclers recorded did not stem from their macabre imagination, but was once reality—even if such gruesome events did not take place at the time the poets and historians were writing about them. If they had witnessed such events at close hand, they wouldn't have been able to write about them anyway, for they would all have been dead. The chroniclers were not eye-witnesses; they wrote down things which others had seen, or heard of, from far away, and then told their offspring, perhaps after visiting the burned lands and cities afflicted by the devastation. Or perhaps after survivors from the outermost fringes of the battle had recounted their appalling experiences to others who had not been involved.

Information of that kind, passed on Chinese-whisper fashion, can never be exact. And even less so given the fact that neither the eyewitnesses nor the later chroniclers had the faintest clue about modern weapons systems. What else could they do but ascribe what they did not understand to supernatural deities? In their eyes they were, after all, "gods"—for what else could they be? There is also a quite clear distinction throughout ancient literature between natural phenomena and the weapons of the gods.

In his *Theogony*, Hesiod also turns his attention to the Cyclops. These were supposed to have been huge figures similar to the gods, who had only one eye in the middle of their foreheads, which gave them their name of "round-eye": "Their single eye was round as a circle and set in the midst of their face."[27]

One might think that Cyclops must really be the products of imagination, since there have never ever been one-eyed creatures, but I'm not so sure. Since the 17th century, there have been documented cases of occasional miscarried fetuses with one eye. And modem genetics has ascertained that only a single gene is responsible for our two eyes. At the earliest fetal stage of vertebrates, to which we belong, there first develops a kind of strip of light-sensitive cells. If the function of the "Pax-6" gene did not kick in, this light-sensitive conglomeration would fail to divide into two separate areas, and we would all be Cyclops. Heaven knows what genetic experiments the gods dreamed up—and where the chroniclers got their idea of the Cyclops from.

The Greek Hesiod also mentions flying chariots in several passages, such as Fragment 30, where Zeus descends with thunder and lightning from the firmament. And the former ruler of Lydia is said to have had access to fairly mind-boggling technology. He was called Gyges and was originally a shepherd. Herodotus writes that Gyges had come, while still young, to Candaules' palace, and had made friends with this ruler. One day Candaules had urged Gyges to hide himself in his bedroom so as to admire the beauty of his wife as she undressed. This happened, but the ruler's wife noticed the voyeur and the next day demanded that he murder her husband, for otherwise she would reveal to all and sundry what had happened, and Gyges would lose his life. If he did murder Candaules she would make him king of Lydia—which is what happened. Now Gyges is said to have possessed a machine which rendered him invisible. Plato writes about this in his dialogue *The State*. When Gyges was still a shepherd, a great storm and earthquake had one day erupted, and the earth had gaped open. Astonished, the young Gyges had stared into a great hole in the ground that appeared before him. He climbed into it and:

> Saw, besides other wonderful things, also a hollow iron horse with windows. Gyges looked in and also saw a corpse within, seemingly bigger than human size. It had nothing on other than a golden ring on one hand, which Gyges drew off and then climbed out again.[28]

The ring could move, and Gyges turned it. When he met his fellow shepherds again, he suddenly noticed that they did not see him. Depending on which way he turned the ring, he either became visible or invisible, but even when invisible he could still hear and see everything going on around him. This amazing ring must have made it very tempting to go and inspect his queen's sleeping quarters. But he must have made some slip for she would not have noticed him otherwise. And for someone who could make himself invisible at will it could not have been too hard to become Lydia's ruler.

The Gyges tale is the oldest known story about a voyeur. It might be pure fantasy, for who wouldn't occasionally like to have a way of becoming invisible? But why all the business with an underground chamber containing the skeleton of a giant, and a metal horse with windows? Somehow this story reminds one of Aladdin, who only had to rub his wonderful lamp, in order to get his heart's desire.

Fairy tales are fairy tales because fictional things take place in them. The accounts of appalling weapons used in prehistoric times do not resemble them in the least, for one thing because they describe a technology which we only now recognize; secondly because fairy-tales would not have been engraved on clay tablets millennia ago, for reasons I have already given; and thirdly because these gods' weapons do not appear in the accounts of only one people or nation.

There is still a further reason why the substance of the *Argonautica* story did not first arise in Greece: constellations. East of the Great Dog constellation—easy to find in the night sky because bright Sirius belongs to it—we also find the Argo cluster. The Argo or "heaven's ship" is relatively difficult to make out, because it lies quite low in the south and in spring vanishes again in the evening. The Argo is said to have been affixed to the firmament by the goddess Athene, who also made the Argonauts' vessel unsinkable, and equipped it with the speaking beam. But this constellation was already known as "heaven's ship" by the ancient Babylonians.[29] The same is true of Aries. The Greeks derived the Aries constellation from the Golden Fleece. They believed that Phrixus and his sister Helle had once flown upon the Golden Fleece from Europe to Asia. Helle fell from the Golden Fleece down into the sea, which is why the channel there is called the Hellespont. The ram (Aries) however, had freed himself from his golden skin and had flown up to the firmament, where he became a constellation. Yet Aries had likewise long been known by the Babylonians.

According to legend, Pegasus, the flying Greek horse, bore upon his back the demonic Chimaera, which had the heads of a lion, goat, and dragon. But this constellation, too, existed millennia before Apollonius. The same is true of the Taurus constellation and the Pleiades. It is easy to show that the Greek poets took their constellations from older peoples, and only later invested them with their own heroes. We can be sure of this simply because some things which the Greeks adopted were no longer applicable even in their own time. For example, in Hesiod's book *Works and Days*, he warns of the 40 days in which the Pleiades are not visible as being a time to avoid travelling by ship. He says that the period of their disappearance is always accompanied in the Mediterranean region by wild storms at sea (the so-called equinox storms). But from an astronomical point of view this was no longer correct in Hesiod's time.

In reality it "applied in 4000 to 2000 BC, at a time when the heliacal setting of the Pleiades fell roughly in the weeks following the spring equinox."[30] So Hesiod must have been drawing on older sources.

The heroes of the *Argonautica* sail down the Eridanos River, which modem scholars try to place in northern Italy. But the Greek texts continually connect this Eridanos with the constellations of Aquarius and Orion. The star-gazers of ancient Babylon saw it in just the same way, which is proved by an astronomical table that was discovered in the clay tablet library of Assurpanibal. And where does the dragon come from that was also admired in the firmament long before the Greek poets arrived on the scene? It appears in Sumerian clay tablets. Some god or other is said to have shown a priest star constellations and even to have drawn them on a tablet. Among these was the heavenly dragon with his many heads. This immediately reminds me of the so-called "heavenly journeys" which the antediluvian prophet Enoch undertook. There too, it was an "angel" who mapped out the firmament for him: "I saw the stars of heaven, and I saw how he called them all by name. I saw how they were weighed in a just scale, according to the strength of their light, after the fashion of their breadth and the day of their appearance."[31]

The world of Greek legend was always related to the fixed stars, but the starry constellations, together with the enigmatic stories and ideas associated with them, existed millennia before then. Prometheus was said to have taught mankind to observe the rising and setting of the stars. He also taught them writing and various branches of knowledge and science. I have already described the sea creature Oannes, who did exactly the same thing. Diodorus of Sicily recounts something very similar in his first book, namely that the first human beings learned their language, writing, and knowledge from the gods.[32] One finds just the same thing amongst the ancient Egyptians,[33] the Japanese,[34] the Tibetans,[35] the Mayans, the Incas....

Only our culture is uninterested in these ancient traditions and accounts. Of course, we know better!

There is not the slightest doubt that the Greek poets and historians took ancient stories and related their versions of them to their own land to "make them their own," investing them with Greek gods and Greek landscapes. But the substance of these stories, whether in the *Argonautica*, or in Hesiod's accounts of the battle between gods and Titans, does not refer to Greece at all. Nevertheless I believe that the descendants of the gods did leave their traces behind in the geographical region of ancient Greece. Let us now see what these traces might be.

Chapter 3
The Network of the Gods

There is no such thing as indisputable truth—
and if there was it would be boring.

—Theodor Fontane, 1819–1898

Egyptology tells us that the Egyptians were the first people to build pyramids. The oldest of all types of pyramid is said to be the step pyramid of Sakkara, built for the Pharaoh Djoser (2609–2590 BC). But is that right?

Pausanius was a Greek travel writer who lived about 1,800 years ago. He travelled about his homeland and wrote vivid, often flowery descriptions of the Greece of his time. One day he was on his way to Epidaurus from Argos, a town not far from the Bay of Nauplia, when he saw a small pyramid to the right of the road (the old road from Argos to Tegea). A little further, no more than half a mile west of the present village of Ligurio, right at the foot of the Arachneus mountain, stood a second pyramid. Pausanius examined the exterior of these pyramids. They were built of hefty blocks of stone, roughly 5 feet (1.5m) long. A few larger chunks lay about on the ground, and Pausanius thought that these must have been grave pyramids.[1]

Not until 1936 and 1937 did archaeologists follow Pausanius' trail and find the pyramids, which today are called the "pyramids of Argolis." Not far from them a megalithic structure was also discovered, which is referred to rather dismissively as a "block house." This is a square structure, built of dressed stone beams. Parts of its construction are reminiscent of the gigantic walls one can find in faraway Peru. At both places, the stonework is not composed of monoliths cut at a right angle, but of blocks interjoined in a complicated fashion, with many corners—secure against earthquakes.

The exterior measurements of the pyramids at Ligurio are as follows: north side 46 feet (14m); west side 41 feet (12.5m); south side 39.5 feet (12m); and east side 42 feet (12.75m). The height is about 33 feet (10m), but the apex is missing. Neither graves nor signs of them were found within, but rather a labyrinth of walls with smaller rooms and what were clearly water tanks. Whether these basins served as baths, and whether there had ever been water in them, could not be proved. The archaeologists of the 1940s dated both pyramids to about 400 BC,[2] and came to the conclusion that they cannot have been either graves or signal towers. Perhaps they were a kind of guardhouse, from where a few soldiers could watch the street. But why did they need to have a pyramid shape? There would have been little point in that since soldiers would no doubt have preferred a platform from which to oversee the region.

In 1997, a Greek-British team once more tackled the pyramids of Argolis. This time they were dated by means of thermoluminescence. (Quartz, calcite, or feldspar radiates light when heated, which allows radioactive impurities in the crystal to be recorded and dated.) The result astonished the experts. The pyramids were at least 4,700 years old—and could have been even older.[3] Even the lowest limit of 2700 BC would make these pyramids older than that of Sakkara.

In the meantime Greek archaeologists have found another, much larger pyramid, not far from Mycenae. This is thought to be millennia older than the Sakkara pyramid. Unfortunately the Ministry of Culture in Athens will not allow this pyramid to be examined more carefully, let alone be excavated. So all that one has is confidential information—from a highly reliable source—which one is not allowed to reveal.

Pausanius was on his way to Epidaurus, which had once been a magnificent shrine to Asclepius. Although Epidaurus is only a few miles from the Aegean Sea, one can see nothing from the shore because it is in the midst of wooded hills. The area of Epidaurus was honored as holy ground 4,000 years ago. Archaeologists have found the remains of temples dedicated to the god Maleatas, who is said to have healed people of their illnesses. The remains of ancient megalithic structures were also found there. Since the different Greek shrines and places of ancient worship which I want to discuss here all have something to do with each other, and because my detective work starts with the structure of the building stones, I would ask my readers to remember the following: the region where Epidaurus developed, in honor of Asclepius, was already a holy place in Stone Age times.

In about the 7th century BC, after more and more people had begun making pilgrimages to Epidaurus, it was dedicated to Asclepius. He was a son of Apollo, that offspring of the gods whose flying vessel had overtaken the Argo on its way to the land of the Hyperboreans. Asclepius was said to have been killed in the name of Zeus, by a bolt of lightning. What terrible thing had he done? Nevertheless, he was still a son of Apollo, who was in turn a son of Zeus, making Zeus his grandfather. The legend tells that after Asclepius had healed many thousands of people, he became overconfident and began bringing people back to life. This angered Zeus so much that he ordered Asclepius to be killed. There are other versions of Asclepius' death, but the Greek authors all agree about one thing: that Asclepius was brought up by the centaur Chiron. This was the same "horse-man" with whom Jason of the Argonauts spent his youth.

The symbol of Asclepius was a snake winding itself around a staff, which still today is the sign of doctors and chemists (and is more commonly known as the Mercury staff).

Present-day Epidaurus is also worth a visit. It is true that most of the ruins date back to the 4th century BC, but the traveller can also find remains of megalithic buildings. The great slabs lie unobtrusively in the surrounding area, or have blended into the terrain. In the center of the site stand the remains of a round building, whose original purpose is unknown. In ancient times the circular hole and polished slabs of stone surrounding it was called the "grave of Asclepius." Later on, it is said, the "holy snakes" of Asclepius were pampered here; and nowadays slightly desperate tour guides speak of a labyrinth, one thing it is certainly not. At the moment Epidaurus is being restored and renovated, and when such work has been completed it is always hard to detect what was there originally.

Image 6: The shrine at Epidaurus dates back to mythical times.

Image 7: This is how the Asclepius temple in Epidaurus is thought
to have once looked.

Image 8: Parts of the temple of Epidaurus show megalithic stone work.

Image 9: The renovated amphitheatre of Epidaurus has perfect acoustics.

So what is supposed to have taken place in Epidaurus millennia ago? A procession of sick people, or victims of accident or war, made their pilgrimage week after week to this ancient place of healing. When they got there they found an inn with 1,150 rooms, as well as several temples, public baths, a sports field, and later a theatre too, with 20,000 seats. Today this theatre has been restored, and the acoustics are still so perfect that tourists sitting in the uppermost row can hear every word which their tour guide speaks (in a normal voice), as he stands below on the "stage." The central site, where healings took place, was called Abaton ("the place that cannot be entered").[4] After the patients had handed their offerings to the priests and participated in a ceremony, they were commanded to go into the "healing sleep." This took place in the Abaton, a hall 262 feet (80m) in length, where miraculous healings regularly occurred. And how do we know this 2,500 years later? The people who had been healed commissioned scribes to immortalize the event and their thanks to the gods in stone and marble tablets. Today many of these still hang in their original positions, while others can be seen in the little museum at Epidaurus. Several of them were found on the floor of the Abaton during excavations in 1882 and 1928. What kind of healing or miracle is supposed to have taken place here? Here are some excerpts from the inscriptions:

> Ambrosia of Athens, one-eyed. Came to plead for help from the god. As she walked about the shrine she laughed and thought it impossible that lame and blind people could be cured. After sleeping in the room of healing she came forth with two good eyes.

> Euhippos carried a spear point around in his knee for six years... when day came he was healed.

> Hermodicos of Lampsacos, lame of body. Asclepius healed him as he slept in the room of healing. He commanded him, when he came out, to bring the largest stone he could find to the shrine. He brought the one which now lies before the shrine.

> Alcetas of Halieis. He was blind and slept in the shrine. When day came he was cured.

Arates of Laconia, dropsy. On her behalf her mother slept while she herself was still in Lacedemon, and saw a dream.... When she returned to Lacedemon, her daughter was cured. She too had seen the same dream.

Euphanes, a child from Epidaurus, suffered from a stone. While he slept, the god asked in a dream: "What will you give me if I heal you?" The child replied: "Ten marbles." The god laughed and promised to heal him. Next day Euphanes was cured.

Aishines climbed a tree to look through the window into the Abaton. He fell down upon a sharp stump and destroyed both his eyes. Blind, he ran into the Abaton and begged the god to help. He was healed.

Aristocritos from Halieis. His boy had swum out to sea, and could not get back. His father, who could not find the boy, slept in the healing room of Asclepius. When he came out, he found the boy unharmed.[5]

Roughly 70 supernatural healings are recorded on these tablets at Epidaurus. One might say there's nothing special about that, for such healing also happens today—for instance at places of Catholic pilgrimage like Lourdes in France or Fatima in Portugal. The people healed by such miracles do not behave any differently nowadays than they did millennia ago. Their gratitude takes the same form and has the same quality, as is proved by the thousands of votive tablets to be found in all places of pilgrimage in the world.

But there is a difference between the miracle healings before Christ, and those of today. Anyone who is miraculously healed nowadays is convinced that Jesus, Mary, or at least a Christian saint has had something to do with it. In Epidaurus there were no Christian figures to whom one could turn for help. So who or what brought about the healing? It is clear that Christian belief is not necessary for a spontaneous and miraculous healing to occur. In Epidaurus, people believed in Apollo and Asclepius, and they were still cured.

So what remains is the belief, the deep inner conviction, which facilitates healing. In all the places of healing, in whatever age, auto-suggestion is paramount, but also mass-hypnosis. Nowadays people pray together, take part in a procession, participate in a religious service together. Formerly they carried out sacrificial rites together, inhaled scents (nowadays it is incense), played flutes (nowadays church organs), or took part in shared worship of some kind. What is important is for thoughts to become focused on a single point, so that consciousness no longer perceives its surroundings or its daily cares and worries. This is called autogenous training or meditation today, but such regulating of thoughts is very ancient and widespread, and is practiced in many religions.

In every place where such activity takes place today, the crowds of worshippers focus upon one single point—the altar or statue of the Madonna. The overall level of consciousness is lowered and people enter a kind of "hypnotic absence." This group experience can be felt by everyone. The longing for a miracle makes people who are otherwise completely different relate to each other, even those wary of crying and howling out loud; all inhibitions disappear. I have often observed this: participants in the daily procession to Lourdes open themselves up to a deep feeling of trust. Here, at the end of their journey, the place they have been longing to reach, they wish to be rid of their suffering. In all religions these almost ecstatic emotions provide the seedbed upon which the unthinkable can take root and become possible.

In Epidaurus it became possible—this is proved by the votive tablets. The priest-doctors were familiar with the suggestive power of the subconscious. Yet it was not priests who first made the pilgrimage to Epidaurus, but human beings. Their increasing numbers made Epidaurus into a place of pilgrimage, and the priests only arrived after this influx had grown to large proportions. This is how I see it: something unbelievable happened at some point in the region of Epidaurus. A "god" descended from the heavens. Only a few people observed this event, and were afraid. But the "god" saw them nevertheless and, without frightening them further, laid small gifts at the edge of the clearing. After initially hesitating, the people fetched these gifts and returned the compliment with presents for the "god." Later such gifts came to be known as "offerings."

Some of the people were ill, and the "god" noticed this. Meanwhile the people had gained trust, and the "god" began to heal their sick. This quickly made the rounds, was spread by word of mouth, so that even long after the "god" had left again, sick people still kept streaming to this extraordinary place. Temples were built, and auto-suggestion played its part. It is not impossible that the "god" left behind some technical apparatus, or sank it into the ground, so as to be able to observe things from a distance and perhaps even influence what went on. It also seems as if this "god" knew how the human brain functions, and what consciousness is capable of.

Epidaurus is still a curious place today. Mobile phones don't work there, or only with difficulty, and the state television company had to set up a good number of amplifiers in the area in order to guarantee a clear reception. Beyond the archaeological zone new hotels have been built for those wishing to be healed, and even the late French president Francois Mitterrand made a secret pilgrimage to Epidaurus to plead for his health. We do not know to which god he directed his prayers.

The next place of activity of the gods' offspring which I would like to examine briefly is Crete. The history of this Mediterranean island has some connection with technology, and it was the site of various inventions. I have already described how the king's daughter Europa is said to have fallen in love with a bull, who was really Zeus, and who swam with the princess straight for Crete. There Zeus had three sons with his beloved, one of whom was called Minos. He became king of Crete, and every nine years received new laws from his father Zeus—a rather good way of keeping up with the times, and being a model for other nations. Minos had a mighty palace built, greater than the world had ever seen before. And of course, being a son of the gods, he took a wife from the race of gods, the daughter of the sun god Helios.

One day Minos decided to make an offering, and the sea god Poseidon sent a beautiful young bull that was really meant for sacrifice. But Minos kept the bull and slaughtered another one. That made Poseidon furious, and he wanted revenge—for the gods' offspring were not all bosom pals. Somehow or other, Poseidon got Minos' wife to fall in love with the bull—an appalling thought.[6] Understandably Minos' wife had to keep quiet about her perverse love, which is why she commissioned a brilliant engineer who lived on Crete to manufacture an artificial cow. The engineer's name was Daedalus, and he constructed such a perfect cow that the queen could place herself inside it, and the fine bull didn't notice that she was there. The bull mated the cow, and soon afterwards the queen felt great pains inside her. She gave birth to a cross-breed, a creature with a human body and the head of a bull. And because the lady was the wife of King Minos, this creature was called the Minotaur (literally "Minos bull").

Minos must have been extremely displeased, for he got Daedalus to construct a giant prison for the Minotaur, a labyrinth of such complexity that no one could get out of it. But this bull-human monster had dreadful desires. Every year seven youths and seven maidens were sent into the labyrinth so that the Minotaur could eat them. Eventually Theseus, the son of the king of Athens, decided to kill the monster and bring this human sacrifice to an end. He voluntarily offered himself as one of the seven youths and journeyed to Crete, where he fell in love with Ariadne, a daughter of Minos. She also asked Daedalus for help, so that her lover might find his way out of the labyrinth again after killing the Minotaur. Daedalus, who had a solution for every problem, showed the king's daughter the labyrinth's exit and gave her a ball of thread, the famous "Ariadne's thread." Her lover had to tie one end of this thread to the entrance when he went in, and unroll it as he went, so that he would then be able to find his way out again.

The rest of the story is quickly told. Theseus killed the Minotaur. King Minos naturally got wind of the role Daedalus had played in the matter, and so threw Daedalus and his son Icarus into jail. Daedalus built himself two winged contraptions out of wood, feathers, resin, and other materials. Daedalus and his son Icarus took flight and rose happily into the air above Crete, but unfortunately the son forgot his father's warning not to fly too close to the sun, for then the resin would melt and the feathers would bum. This is exactly what happened—the young man plummeted down, and since then the sea where he fell has been called the Sea of Icarus. The island where his body was washed ashore is called Icaria.

Daedalus flew on to Sicily, where the king enthusiastically adopted this engineering genius. After all, every ruler wishes to have the technological edge over other countries. But Minos was in a rage because Daedalus had left. He went with his fleet to search the whole Mediterranean, and finally found Daedalus on Sicily; but the king of Sicily did not want to hand him over. Instead, the king's daughters boiled Minos alive in a bathtub. There are Greek legends which say that the body of King Minos was brought back to Crete and buried there.

Of course, things never happened exactly as the myth tells. The Greek archaeologist Anna Michailidou believes she has dismissed any such idea: "The myth has absolutely no basis in historical reality."[7] All the famous poets and historians of ancient Greece have written about the Cretan myths: Homer, Hesiod, Thucydides, Pindar, Plutarch, Diodoros of Sicily, and of course Herodotus. Each of them gives different variations and angles, so that only the basic story remains the same.

No labyrinth has ever been found on Crete, unless the palace of King Minos was implied, for the "House of Minos" at Knossos was bigger than Buckingham Palace, and contained roughly 1,400 rooms on several floors. One could certainly have got lost there.

In the middle of the 19th century this giant complex was just an insignificant-looking hill. Not until 1878 did a Greek, Minos Kalokairinis, begin some modest excavations in Knossos. Then in 1894, the British archaeologist Arthur Evans (1851–1941) came to Crete. Just like Heinrich Schliemann, he believed in the reality of Homer's writings. Homer had given very detailed accounts of the Cretan legends and provided clear descriptions of the palace of Knossos.

Arthur Evans first returned to England and was promoted to Director of the Ashmolean Museum in Oxford. Here he collected funds and patrons so as to be able to excavate on Crete. He finally started to dig with a team of 30 on March 23, 1900, and the excavators gradually revealed layer upon layer of King Minos' legendary palace.

Image 10: Hundreds of clay vessels of Knossos were buried in the earth. Did they once contain fuel oil for the "flying tubs" of the gods' offspring?

Image 11: Clay vessels of Knossos.

Image 12: Clay vessels of Knossos.

Image 13: The foundations of King Minos' palace on Crete go back to megalithic times.

Image 14: The remains of the palace of Knossos on Crete.

Image 15: The restored hall of the palace of Knossos on Crete.

One thing became immediately clear: there had been a bull cult here. Bull images were found on wall-paintings and clay fragments, and bull horns were depicted everywhere. Nothing of a technical nature was found—no workshop of the brilliant Daedalus, no bones of a Minotaur, and sadly no single metal piece of the Talos robot from the *Argonautica.* That's probably rusting away under the water in one of Crete's thousands of bays.

The whole island lacked any defenses—no walled towns or castles, and no defensive walls against invaders from the sea. So did they rely on the Talos robot? Despite this, Arthur Evans was able to prove that Homer's descriptions had been very accurate. What surprised the excavators most of all was the great age of their finds. The palace of Knossos had been destroyed and rebuilt several times, but even the earliest one had been the same size as the most recent. The oldest palace remains dated back to 3000 BC, and every new layer that was exposed led further and further back to the Stone Age. Finally, it became clear that people had lived on the site 8,000 years ago, before the palace of Knossos was ever built. What had been so special about this site? Megalithic remains were discovered too—not only in Knossos but scattered amongst diverse temple complexes.

The buildings of the Knossos palace turned out to be an interconnected complex of inner courtyards, rooms, small chambers, and low doors. There were also bath-shaped vessels with waste-plug holes—but without any pipes leading away from them. Finally there was an astonishing number of steps and stairs: three sets lay only 33 feet (10m) distant from one another on the same wing, and led to a large roof terrace. Was there some reason why all the inhabitants might need to get up to the roof at the same time? Arthur Evans found many store and stockrooms, filled with clay vessels the size of two men. Professor Dr. H. G. Wunderlich wrote about this:

> Even with "normal size" storage vessels one has to wonder how they were ever emptied and cleaned from time to time, since one would hardly be able to reach the bottom of them even with very long ladles, and even if one stood on a chair or stool. The giant Pithoi [stone vessels] provide us with an insoluble problem in this

regard: they can't even be tipped on their side.... Storage jars of this size must have been brought and raised before the walls were built which surrounded them, and they could not have then been replaced at any later stage by other jars. Filling and emptying must have taken place by means of tubes, along "communicating tube" principles. Yet how impractical to wall in such vessels in a place so difficult of access! One turns away with some irritation....[8]

Someone worked out that one of these monstrous clay jars contained an average 129 gallons (586 l): "The number of containers in the west wing of the Knossos palace alone comes to 420, which means a storage capacity of 54,180 gallons (246,120 l)."[9]

As well as these clay vessels in the west wing, there were also "oil containers" throughout the whole complex, often called "cisterns" by the archaeologists. They amounted to an enormous storage capacity. And for what reason? One theory is that the Minoans had made provision for times of crisis, but this is unconvincing. Knossos does not appear to have feared any danger, for the whole island was without defenses. The ruler was the son of a god, and could deal with any eventuality; and then there was also the robot Talos who guarded the island. So why should they have wanted to store such absurd quantities of edible oil, which would have soon deteriorated in the Mediterranean heat?

All that we can do is speculate, and try to find a possible solution. A few years ago, I turned my attention to King Solomon and the Queen of Sheba.[10] It turned out that Solomon used a flying machine "which he had built in accordance with the wisdom bestowed upon him by God."[11] He also gave such a "chariot which flew through the air" to his queen.

This was not an extraterrestrial vehicle of some kind, but probably a relatively simple construction in the form of a hot-air balloon. Let us not forget that in mythology the sons of the gods received all sorts of technological instruction from their fathers, which gave them the edge over ordinary human beings.

In the accounts, several thousand years old, of Solomon's flying chariot, we also hear that such vehicles required "fire and water." And indeed, curious structures dedicated to Solomon have been found on top of various mountains. These mountain summits are called "Takht-I-Suleiman" or "Throne of Solomon," and they can be found in present-day Kashmir, Iran, and Iraq, and on the Arab peninsula as far as the Yemen. All these structures, and the temples on the mountain summits, were dedicated to the worship of water and fire, and in all of them oil storage places have been found. If Solomon's flying machine had been powered by a primitive steam engine, water and fire would have been needed. But how would Solomon have heated the water in his flying tub? By means of flammable oil, similar to the way the wick lights up in an oil lamp.

So I have good grounds for asking the rather provocative question: Were the oil reserves in the Knossos palace fuel-oil stores? Did everyone rush out together on to the roofs because a flying vehicle was arriving? There is evidence to support this idea; in the sixth book of his Natural History, the Roman historian Pliny the Elder, who lost his life in the eruption of Vesuvius in the year AD 79, recounts the following about the peoples living in Arabia: "However the [most] royal residence of all is Mariaba[12].... In the interior of the country the Minaens border on the Atramites. The former are thought to descend from the Cretan king Minos."[13]

And in the twelfth book Pliny turns to the varieties of tree in Arabia, and in particular the "incense tree":

> It is bordered by another region in which the Minaens live, through which people pass on a narrow road to carry away incense. This people began this trade, and still pursue it most intensively, which is why it is given the name of "Minaee." Apart from the Minaens, no other Arab sees the incense tree, and not even all of them do. Their number is said to be no more than 3,000 families, who make sure that this right is passed on through the generations.[14]

Things gradually become clearer. The palace of Knossos was continually destroyed and rebuilt over a long period; but around 1500 BC the "Minoans" vanish into thin air and their buildings on Crete are swallowed up in a catastrophe. Up to this point, there were giant stores of oil in the palace. At the same time, a branch of the Minoan people appears in far-off Yemen, and starts to trade in incense. Incense was treated like gold in those days—of which the gods' offspring couldn't get enough. Even in the early days of barter and exchange, artists and workers had to be paid, for no one could just live from hand to mouth. The Queen of Sheba had the largest and most technologically brilliant dam of antiquity built in Marib in the Yemen, and her relatives on Crete had to keep up a gigantic palace, which often collapsed because of earthquakes. Without financial stimulus, none of this could have happened. According to Pliny, the "Minaens" started by trading in incense, which is why this trade is called "Minaee." Pliny doesn't regard these Minaens as traders from Crete, but as Arabs, for he says: "Apart from the Minaens no other Arab sees the incense tree."

Image 16: The dam of Marib (Yemen) was constructed by the queen of Sheba.

Image 17: The dam of Marib.

The Queen of Sheba, for her part, was a successor to King Minos of Crete. He, in turn, was an offspring of the gods, with all the technical know-how his parents had passed on to him. Solomon belonged to the same elevated circle of the wise, which is why—and this is quite clear from Arabian literature—this Biblical ruler had a quite different order of technology at his disposal from that described elsewhere in the Old Testament.[15, 16] After all, his mistress was the Queen of Sheba, whom he visited frequently on his flying machine. When all is said and done this means that the mythical King Minos was, as the legend says, the son of a "god," married to the daughter of the sun-god Helios—the same who unwillingly handed the sun-chariot's reins (or should we say controls?) to his son Phaethon.

The family should be regarded as having technical know-how. On Crete its members consolidated their power and allowed themselves to be pampered by human beings. They built the robot Talos, which guarded the island, and taught the inhabitants how to produce the large quantities of oil which were needed for royal flying machines. A descendant of Minos ruled Arabia and began trading in incense. In Sheba's domain, too, more than average amounts of oil were produced. Thus it is quite feasible that over many generations large sums were shunted backward and forward between the Minoan relatives. They helped themselves to a royal lifestyle, until finally the Cretan branch of the family broke apart. The same happened in Sheba's kingdom. Even the "royal blood" of the "gods" ultimately degenerated, and with it the secret knowledge about earlier technologies.

When exactly all this began can no more be ascertained than the point at which people first started making pilgrimages to the god of healing at Epidaurus. The important thing as I see it is that the "gods" were indeed worshipped already 6,000 years ago, on the same geographical site where Knossos was later built, 3 miles (5 km) southeast of the present town of Iraklion on Crete. This links up with the riddles which I am trying to solve.

North of Crete lies the Anticythera Channel, named after the islands of Cythera and Anticythera. In olden times, when sailors preferred, for safety's sake, to hug the coastline rather than plough out into the midst of the ocean, there were frequent shipwrecks. Sometimes boats crashed into each other in the dark, sometimes fires broke out on board, sometimes pirates or warships took what they could plunder, or vessels sank without trace into the depths. One of these wrecks was discovered by chance by a ship-full of Greek sailors, who had taken refuge from a storm in a bay on the eastern side of Anticythera. They were actually diving for sponges, shells, and pearls at the time, and because they were camped for the night on Anticythera's beach, they thought they might do a bit of diving there the next day. At low tide, at a depth of 100 feet (30m), Elias Stadiatis caught sight of a wooden mast and then the bulk of a ship. Excitedly he told his companions, and everyone leapt into the water to see it. This was two days before Easter, 1900. During the following days the men brought more and more objects to the surface, and finally told the authorities about their discovery.

These were dangerous diving conditions, given the depth of water, which meant that no one could go down more than twice a day. The divers didn't have oxygen cylinders, so it took all their effort just to reach the wreck, cram some object into a basket that was suspended on a rope, then get themselves pulled up quickly again. It is no surprise therefore that two people lost their lives during the diving, and two others became seriously ill.

During several months, figurines, coins, two bronze arms, blue vases, and even small marble statues (later dated at 80 BC) came to light. Finally, one of the men glimpsed something like a square object in the dark water, covered in shells, limestone, and corroding lumps of metal. The diver had no idea what he had found. During the next few days other fragments of it were brought to the surface, but even the archaeologist on board did not at first recognize the significance of this unique find.

In the Greek National Museum in Athens, the formless structure was chemically treated so as to reveal what lay underneath the layers of sediment. The curators were amazed to see three cog-wheels, joined together by two cross-shaped metal strips. Then a tiny cog-wheel just 2mm thick crumbled under the brush of one of the curators. They realized at this point that it was a technical apparatus of some kind, and that they needed specialist help.

Valerio Stais was one of the students who handled the separate cog-wheels with tweezers, laid them out to dry, and treated them with chemical cleaning agents. He later became an archaeologist, and was the first to begin to grasp what lay in front of him in the half-darkened rooms of the Greek National Museum. By that point more than 30 little cog-wheels of varying sizes had come to light, and also some letters in ancient Greek script. The apparatus quite clearly had something to do with astronomy. Valerio Stais said as much to a journalist, and was severely reprimanded by the specialists for doing so.

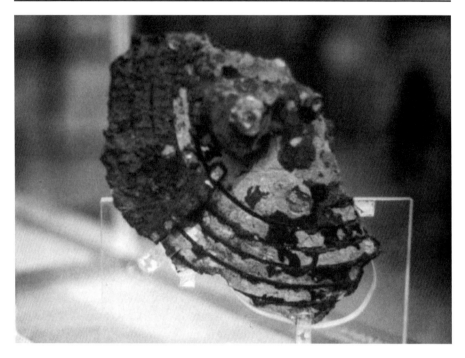

Image 18: The Machine of Anticythera can now be seen in the Greek National Museum in Athens.

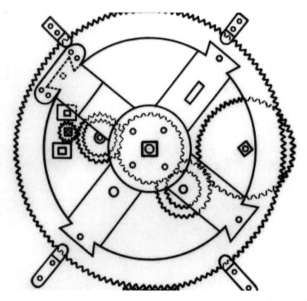

Image 19: The Machine of Anticythera.

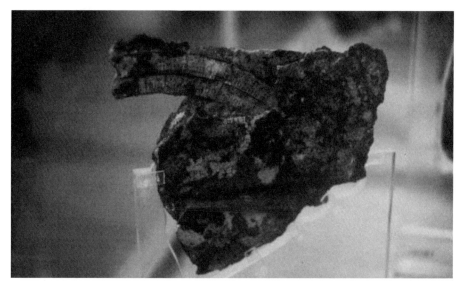

Image 20: The Machine of Anticythera.

In the following years several "specialists"—either genuine or self-appointed—turned their attention to the "Anticythera mechanism" as it had come to be known. As usual they all came up with differing results. In the summer of 1958, 58 years after its discovery, the young English mathematician Dr. Derek J. Solla Price was given permission to examine this disputed piece of antiquity. At last a mathematician who had studied astronomy was allowed to bring his knowledge to bear on it. Dr. Solla Price later became Professor of the History of Science at Yale University. He published the only thorough studies about this machine, and did not disguise his astonishment.[17]

The metal parts consisted of pure bronze or copper-tin alloys in varying compositions. There were also small amounts of gold, nickel, arsenic, sodium, iron, and antimony. The engraved Greek letters, that were only partially decipherable, gave absolutely certain proof that this strange find had an astronomical purpose. There were phrases such as "at evening the Bull"; "Vega sinks at evening"; "the Pleiades appear in the morning." There were also star names and constellations such as "Gemini, Altair, Arcturus." The text was interspersed with single engraved numbers. Finally one could make out three circular measuring rules, with millimeter lines, similar to a slide-rule. More than 30 cogwheels of differing sizes interconnected with one another and were fastened to a copper plate by means of small axles. The mechanism even had differential wheels, which obviously allowed the relationships between different star positions to be read off on the scale. This sounds complicated, but is not necessarily—for example, when the Pleiades rise, where does the star Altair stand? The mechanism also allowed the moon's positions in relation to the sun and the earth to be calculated, or the rising and setting of Sirius in comparison to Vega.

The Anticythera mechanism had obviously been made a few hundred years BC. Yet it must have been built in a secret laboratory, for the knowledge which went into making it was quite unknown in those times. The same applies to the level of technology and fine mechanics invested in it. Professor Solla Price occupied himself with this machine for years, and once said in a lecture in Washington that the whole thing seemed as strange to him as if a can-opener had been found among the treasures of Tutankhamun. Yet Solla Price of course knew all about the achievements of the great ancient Greek mathematicians and philosophers, such as Aristotle (born 384 BC) or Archimedes (born 285 BC). It is also known that the Arabs had outstanding astronomers and built mechanically functioning calendars, so-called astrolabes, around about AD 1000. But none of this could explain the knowledge which went into making the Anticythera mechanism. Let me quote Solla Price:

> Either the Anticythera mechanism represents a cutting-edge sequence of scientific development which has never been written about, or it is the brain-child of an extraordinary, unknown genius. Even if one makes enormous allowances for the date of this machine, it must be clear that we have here something much more complicated than was ever mentioned in ancient literature.[18]

Professor Solla Price was the only person to devote years of study to this extraordinary machine, and in the process he investigated all ancient writings about mechanics, mathematics and astronomy. At the end of his investigations he wrote, "The Anticythera mechanism confronts us with a phenomenon of a quite different order: it is High Technology, a term we use to describe special advances in science."

The Anticythera mechanism was kept out of the public eye for nearly 90 years. Recently several separate parts of it have been placed on view in a glass cabinet in the Greek National Museum. This apparatus, now illumined by spotlights, tells us how little we know about the wisdom which the gods whispered into the ears of their darlings. It also demonstrates the dull, lazy habits of thought of the herd mentality in our society. Here we have a high-tech gadget with cogwheels, with up to 240 teeth, which can measure up to a hundredth of a millimeter. If the differentials were any greater, the scale of measurement would be imprecise or wrong. This technical miracle is not mentioned anywhere in ancient literature, although it must have been the talk of the town when it first appeared. Where are its forerunners? These must have existed, for even the greatest genius of fine mechanics could not have constructed such a thing "from cold." And if earlier models existed, why are they not mentioned by any poets or historians of the time, who took such pains to record everything else? (There were later versions of this kind of machine, but with a much simpler mechanical construction—but that's another story.) And where did the astronomical knowledge come from which underpins this miracle? People peer into the glass case in the Greek National Museum in Athens and think, "Oh well, those ancients must have done it somehow. Geniuses don't just fall out of the sky."

The Anticythera mechanism was made in portable size, something like a typewriter. It could easily have been transported from one "god's" palace to another. It could also have served useful purposes on board one of the flying machines of prehistory. The flying Solomon, like the Indian royal families who likewise mastered air travel,[19] doubtless needed navigational instruments. So it is not surprising to find Arabian historians telling us that, in his "chariot which flew through the air," Solomon used a "magic mirror which revealed to him all places on the earth."[20] This miraculous object was "composed of various substances," and enabled the king on his flying carpet to "see into all seven climates." And Abdul Al-Mas'udi (AD 895–956), the Arab world's most important geographer and historian, wrote in his *Histories*[21] that, on the mountaintops where Solomon clearly refueled, there were wonderful walls which showed Solomon the "heavenly bodies, the stars, the earth with its continents and seas, the inhabited regions, their plants and animals, and many astonishing things."[22] They were no doubt at least as astonishing as the Anticythera mechanism.

North of the islands of Anticythera and Cythera lies the Peloponnese, at 8,266 square miles (21,410 sq km), the largest Greek peninsula. Here are the towns of Argos, Epidaurus, and Nemea, and between them the very ancient Mycenae. As everywhere else in Greece, Mycenae is inseparable from mythology. The place is said to have been founded by Perseus, whose mother claimed he was the son of Zeus—who seems to have been responsible for every unusual child. Perseus' huge fame is based on his defeat of the Gorgons, horrible monsters with several heads. They were supposed to have had hands of brass and wings of gold, and anyone who looked at their face was immediately turned to stone. One of these Gorgons was Medusa, who still embodies the feminine's most nightmarish aspect, and she was the one on whom Perseus used a divine trick or two to in order to kill her. From the nymphs he received a special pouch, which he threw over his shoulder, a pair of flying sandals, and a helmet which made him invisible. Then the god Hermes turned up and handed Perseus the ultimate weapon: a diamond sickle. Thus armed, Perseus flew to the Gorgons' stronghold, making sure to stare only at his polished shield, which shone like a mirror. By doing so, he avoided all direct eye-contact, and escaped being turned to stone. Since he was invisible, the dreadful monsters did not notice him, and our brave hero struck off Medusa's head.

Taking the head of this horror with him, Perseus first flew to Egypt, where two of his elders lived, then on to Ethiopia. A king there had been forced to sacrifice his own lovely daughter Andromeda to a sea monster. Naturally, Perseus soon dealt with this underwater beast and, after an intrigue or two, finally got his Andromeda. In the meantime, his friends in Ethiopia were facing attack from a great power. "I'll soon sort this out," said Perseus to himself, and, telling his friends to cover their eyes, he fetched Medusa's head from his special rucksack and turned it on his enemies, at which they all turned to stone. Perseus used this secret weapon again on another occasion. (It might be of interest to compare this with the account in the *Kebra Negest,* the story of Ethiopia's royal family, in which thousands of soldiers die in a mysterious fashion because they gaze upon the Ark of the Covenant, which Solomon's son had stolen in Jerusalem and transported to Ethiopia.) Later Perseus returned with Andromeda to his home territory of Argolis, and eventually founded the town of Mycenae. But of course there are other stories about Perseus as well.

No one knows exactly when Mycenae was first inhabited, but we are sure of one thing: that it was at some point in the Stone Age. The surrounding landscape is mountainous, and the Argolis Mountains soon started to be mined for copper ore. We will never know whether copper was the reason for people coming to live there, or whether there was another, "holy" reason. What has been proven archaeologically is that megalithic structures were built here already 2,500 years BC, and that 1,000 years later Mycenae had mighty defenses of great, 20-foot (6m) thick walls.

Mycenae also plays an important role in Homer's tale of Troy, although we still do not know where the poet drew his information from. According to Homer, the heroes of the Trojan War, Agamemnon and his companions, are supposed to be buried in Mycenae. This is why Heinrich Schliemann dug in Mycenae. In five grave chambers he found the skeletons of 12 men, three women, and two children. And because the graves were richly endowed with gold, Schliemann immediately sent a telegram to the Greek king in Athens and claimed that these treasures alone would be enough to fill a large museum. That was overly optimistic: his finds can today be admired in one room of the Greek National Museum.

Image 21: The megalithic walls of Mycenae.

Image 22: The megalithic walls of Mycenae.

Image 23 and 24: It seems as if the stone blocks of Mycenae were molded from various different materials.

*Image 25: The entrance and dome of the Treasure House of Atreus at Mycenae.
No one knows what was once stored there.*

Mycenae is also worth a visit for the tourist. One can see the Cyclops Wall, so-called because according to legend it was built by the one-eyed monsters. Midway along the wall, resting on three monoliths, is the Lion Gate. And every visitor who sits and eats his sandwiches in the shadow of the walls ought really to notice something strange: many of the stones of which the Cyclops Wall is built cannot be purely natural stone, because they consist of a variety of materials. It is just as if coarse concrete had once been mixed here. This Cyclops wall is about 985 yards (900m) long, and above and below it are smaller walls dating from a later period.

A few hundred yards lower down lies the so-called Treasure House of Atreus, a truly impressive building that is once supposed to have served as a monument, although I have my doubts whether this was its original purpose. The mighty domed structure, which lies underneath a hill, has a diameter of 49 feet (15m) and a height of 43 feet (13.3m). The arch of the dome has been constructed in 33 overlapping layers, each succeeding one projecting a little farther than the one beneath, until finally a huge block of stone closes the hole at the top of the dome. The entrance stone weighs all of 120,000 kilos, and statisticians have worked out that the cupola could easily bear a weight of 140 tons. Unfortunately, no one knows what may originally have lain inside this huge hall; robbers had done their work long before the archaeologists arrived.

Mycenae was strongly linked with Crete at a very early stage. This is proved by Minoan paintings and jewelry found in Mycenae. The gods' descendants from Crete had a hand in the affairs of Mycenae; I am not talking about the later Minoan influences, through cultural exchange, but rather of the original Mycenae settlement. This played a particular role in the network whose threads I am slowly drawing together.

The Greek cult sites are all part of a single, astonishing framework. To make this absolutely clear, I would have to describe many of these sites in detail and assign them to their gods, but this would go beyond the scope of this book. We have so far dealt with four major places: Knossos, Epidauros, Mycenae, and Olympia. The last has not yet been ascribed its god. We still need to mention at least two holy places to fill out the picture: Athens and Delphi.

I did briefly mention that competitions took place in Olympia before the first Olympic games were ever held. Like all the other sites, the region of Olympia was already settled in the Stone Age. The ruins of the temples and sports arenas as one sees them today have largely been restored—yet relics of a former megalithic building style can still be found. This is a point which I cannot repeat often enough: the further back into the past we go, the larger are the building stones which people used—megalithos means "large stone"—as if it wasn't easier to build with smaller stones. This is true all over the world. Clearly, Stone Age people particularly enjoyed heaving giant blocks about, though it does not seem that they had the technology to do so. In later epochs people had humbler aspirations and did not feel the need to exert themselves so much.

Zeus himself was the chief god of Olympia. Whole volumes have been written about him, and so I will limit myself to a lightning survey. The word Zeus—Jupiter to the Romans, Thor to the Germanic tribes—contains the Indo-European root of "dei" or "shining."[23] Even Zeus was not considered by the Greeks to have arisen from nothing, but was a son of Chronus. Hesiod tells us that Chaos originally reigned, an ur-condition out of which the earth, or Gaia, was formed. The earth gave birth to Uranus, the heavens, and from the union between Gaia and Uranus the Titans came forth, as well as Chronos. The latter got his sister pregnant, and one of the offspring of this remarkable pair was Zeus.

The older Zeus became, the more he hated his father Chronus, and finally he fought both him and the Titans. This battle of the gods led Zeus down from Olympus—down from the heights in other words. Zeus won the battle, killed the Titans, but left his father Chronus—who was immortal—alive. Three of Chronus' sons remained: Zeus, Poseidon, and Hades. They divided up their territory between them: Zeus got the heavens, Poseidon the seas and Hades the underworld.

These are the essentials of Zeus' origin, although they don't really tell us very much. The animal symbol of Zeus is the eagle. People gave him names such as the "Thunderer," the "Bolt Hurler," the "Far Sighted," or the "Shape Changer." This last referred to his gift for assuming the guise of different creatures, which he practiced extensively so as to have his way with a whole series of lovely ladies. To Leda he appeared in the shape of a swan, to Europa as a bull, to Calisto as the young Apollo, or—even more exotic—to Danae as golden rain. However, he was also very attracted to beautiful young men, and fell in love with Prince Ganymedes, whom he straightaway abducted to his heavenly kingdom of Olympus. Not the most delicate of divine behavior!

These attributes are the endowments of a mystical superbeing who could do everything, was allowed to do anything, and whom no one understood. Particularly puzzling and incomprehensible is the birth of Athene, a daughter of Zeus. She did not appear via the normal route of a mother's body, but sprang, fully armed, directly from Zeus' forehead. (There are also other versions of her birth.) In mythology she also bears the name of Parthenos, the virgin. Long before the Christian virgin birth, Athene was said to have been born in a similar fashion. Athene, as the name tells us, is the patron goddess of Athens.

She is the very same goddess who helped in building the Argo, and equipped it with a speaking beam. She also helped Perseus in his efforts to strike off the terrible head of the Medusa. Greek legend tells of the famous flying horse Pegasus, who, like Phaethon's sun-chariot, had to be steered, or piloted one might say. Athene also sorted this out by giving the driver "magic reins." She was a most helpful goddess, and was soon promoted to protectress of the arts, wisdom, rhetoric, peace, and also poetry. Maybe I should invoke her! It was also Athene who gave farmers the plough to make their work easier, the loom to women, and the alphabet to the studious.

At some point or other Hephaestus, the god of fire, took great delight in the virginal Athene, and tried by all possible means to get her into his power. Eventually the two fought one another, and the excited Hephaestus lost sperm which dripped on to the soil of a hill at Athens. This was a sufficiently important event for human beings to regard this place as holy ground and build a huge temple site there: the Acropolis.

The present ruins of the Acropolis come from the 6th to the 4th century BC, but in Stone Age times—whenever that was—people already worshipped their gods here. This has been proved by archaeology, for megalithic structures existed on the cliffs above Athens long before the temple buildings arose. Both on the north as well as the south slope, remains of buildings from the Neolithic period have been located. Two of these ancient cult sites were integrated into the later temples. The mightiest monument of the Acropolis is the Parthenon, built on the foundations of an earlier structure. Even today, tourists get their breath literally taken away by the time they reach this temple with its 39-foot (12m) high white marble columns, after an exhausting climb up seemingly endless steps. Parthenon means "virgin chamber," for the temple was dedicated to the virginal Athene. The building is 220 feet (67m) long, 77 feet (23.5m) wide and a full 39 feet (12m) high. On the restored pediment, one can see depicted the birth of Athene, as well as her quarrel with Poseidon, who once wished to take the Acropolis cliffs for himself. Finally there are reliefs of the battles of the gods with the Titans, the battles against the centaurs,

the battle of Troy and—astonishingly enough—the battle of the Athenians
and the Amazons.

   The whole world nowadays complains about the Athens smog corroding the magnificent temple on the Acropolis. And that is quite right. But
who knows why the Parthenon was destroyed back in the 17th century?
After the reign of Emperor Justinian (AD 527–565), Christianity spread
through Greece, and the old temples on the Acropolis were transformed
into churches. Later the Turks arrived to wage war on the Christians,
and stored their gunpowder in the Parthenon. On September 26, 1687, a
Utineburg lieutenant serving in the Venetian forces blew this powder-store
into the air. The explosion tore apart the friezes and columns. Surely even
the last remaining gods must have fled at this barbaric treatment.

Image 26: The Acropolis at Athens.

Image 27: One can also find prehistoric structures at the Acropolis.

Image 28: The Acropolis at Athens.

Image 29: The Acropolis at Athens.

Knossos, Epidaurus, Mycenae, Olympia, the Acropolis—they were all regarded as holy places long before there was a "classical Greece," and millennia before Greek history was written down. We are still missing the "central station" in this network though, and this is more connected with the gods and the history of Greece than all other cult sites. And naturally this nodal point in the network didn't arise by chance, for in myth everything has a cause and reason.

Zeus one day sent two eagles flying around the earth in order to measure it. Wherever the eagles met after their circumnavigation would be the earth's midpoint. Zeus' symbolic creatures met one another again on the steep slopes of a mountain—which was the "omphalos," the navel of the world. And beside the slopes of the mountain later called Parnassus, the mysterious center of the Greek world, Delphi, arose. The etymology of the word "Delphi" is disputed. It may be derived from Delphinios because the god Apollo is said to have come there in the shape of a dolphin; or from Delphys, which means "womb."

Image 30: The plinth of a former pillar at Delphi demonstrates the scale of construction.

Image 31: More massive still is the so-called Polygonal Wall at Delphi, from an unknown epoch.

Delphi is well known for its notorious "oracles," prophecies uttered by a priestess called the Pythia. Even the little word "Pythia" is no accident. In prehistoric times a dragon-snake—another one!—was said to live in the Delphi caves, and was finished off by Apollo, who also journeyed to Delphi in a "heavenly vessel." The terrible dragon was later called "Python," derived from the verb pythein which means to decompose and dissolve. Apollo killed this monster and pushed it back into a cave in the rockface. There it rotted away, and over this spot the "Pythia" was said to have thought up her inspired oracular sayings.

This is no more than folk legend, and is told in many different versions. Every Greek poet and historian wrote about Delphi. The place was, for a long time, the religious center for all Greeks, and it was here that princes and kings came for advice.

In the first book of his *Histories*, Herodotus tells how a certain "Glaucos from Chios, known as the only artist on earth to have found a method of welding iron,"[24] had given Delphi the first welded iron stand. Later things heated up in Delphi. The king of the Lydians, Croisos (now known as Croesus), didn't want to trust the oracle, and therefore sent several different delegations to different oracle sites in Greece. Each oracle was asked the same question: "What am I doing at this moment?" He had made a prior agreement with his messengers about the precise time they would ask this question. When they came back from consulting the different oracles, the only correct answer was the one from Delphi. At the time in question, Croesus had cut up a tortoise, slaughtered a lamb, and cooked both together in an iron pot that was closed by an iron lid. The answer from Delphi went: "Into my senses comes the smell of the armored toad, as it is being cooked together with lamb flesh in an iron pan. Metal holds them below, and metal also shuts them in above."[25]

Image 32: The cone-like stones in Delphi prove the exact measurements.

Image 33: The Treasure House of the Athenians at Delphi.

*Image 34: Sports were also practiced at Delphi. This stadium
once held 4,000 people.*

*Image 35: The foundations of the Apollo Temple at Delphi are
proof of its monumental significance.*

King Croesus was so impressed that he heaped presents on Delphi. He is said to have sacrificed no less than 3,000 head of cattle there, and to have "melted down unending quantities of gold, and had tiles made from it." All were a hand's breadth high and six hands' breadth long, altogether 117 such tiles. This did not seem to be enough though, for he also delivered to Delphi a lion figure of pure gold, as well as two giant mixing pitchers of silver and gold, and jewelry and huge quantities of clothes. Herodotus, who visited Delphi several times, tells us that the golden pitcher stood on the right-hand side of the temple entrance, and the silver one on the left. Later on, he says, two holy water basins which also came from Croesus were engraved with a false inscription. The travelling historian was annoyed about this, 2,500 years ago: "That is not right," he wrote, "for it was really Croesus who donated these [basins]. The inscription was engraved by a man from Delphi. I know the man, but I will not name him."[26]

I have recounted this story to remind you why we speak of someone as "rich as Croesus," and also to demonstrate how wealthy Delphi became. Although King Croesus virtually bought up Delphi wholesale, and en-sured that he always had the right to call up the Pythia, the oracle was no help to him at the critical moment. Croesus was unsure whether he should wage war against the Persians. The Delphian oracle told him that if he crossed the river Halys he would destroy a great kingdom. Such a phrase, open to dual interpretation, could have come from a modem horoscope. In the year 546 BC, King Croesus crossed the Halys, certain of victory—and was wiped out by the Persians. The "great kingdom" which he destroyed was his own.

In the center of Delphi stood the temple of Apollo, which is still an impressive structure today. Apollo, a son of Zeus, had a whole range of abilities. He functioned as god of light and god of medicine. It was not for nothing that Asclepius of Epidaurus was his son. Apollo was in charge of prophecy too, and was also god of youth, music, and shooting with the bow. Apollo's little brother was called Hermes. In ancient Egyptian texts, it says that Hermes was the same as the one whom the Egyptians named Idris or Saurid, but also the one whom the Hebrew people called "Enoch, the son of

Jared."[27] (Even if this is only remotely true, we would be back in the times
before the Great Flood. Saurid is said to have erected the Great Pyramid
before that catastrophe, and Enoch is a Biblical, antediluvian patriarch.)

Remarkably enough, Apollo is also said to have built the unvanquish-
able walls of Troy. He was worshipped as "protector of the ways and
roads," and with his heavenly vessel made regular trips to other peoples,
in particular the Hyperboreans who lived somewhere "beyond the North
winds." Even at Herodotus' time the Greeks did not know who these
ominous-sounding Hyperboreans were. Hesiod and Homer mention them,
and Herodotus finally gives up trying to track them down (IV, 36): "If the
Hyperboreans exist, then there must also be people living in the farthest
reaches of the South. I have to laugh when I see how many people have
drawn maps of the world."

And I have to smile when I think for how many millennia mankind has
been stumbling about in the fog of mythology. These stories may be a great
source of poetry—and all the "gods" offered rich pickings for human fantasy to expand on—but unfortunately they are not true. What remains of
the myths is not datable history, is little upon which to build accurate fact.
Yet they still contain a most decisive and essential core of truth which has
survived all wars and catastrophes in the form of a nebulous folk memory,
which ultimately transforms itself into stone and can be traced at all "mystical" sites. Things are no different nowadays. Places of pilgrimage arise
without exception from little events which someone or other says they
have experienced: a Mary miracle perhaps; or an astonishing, sudden cure;
a spring or an incomprehensible natural phenomenon. Other people, astonished to hear of such a thing, start to visit the site where it happened, out of
curiosity. Then comes the first pub, the first chapel, the first church, always
at the place where something apparently inexplicable occurred. Buildings
arise where folk memory is at work.

Everyone should go and see Delphi. The complex spreads out under
Parnassus, surrounded by the gentle slopes of mountains which at evening
shroud the landscape in cascades of color, light and shadow. Pausanius,
the traveller from 1,800 years ago, describes his impressions in reverent
words, and does not forget to mention the many and disputed tales about

Delphi. Close to 3,000 statues, he says, are said to have flanked the holy street.[28] In his day the "Sayings of the Seven Wise Men" still stood chiseled in stone on the wall of the antechamber of the main temple. They were pieces of wisdom which came from various visitors to Delphi and which still possess relevance today:

- Know thyself.
- Most people are bad.
- Practice makes perfect.
- Seize the day.
- Nothing in excess.
- More haste less speed.
- No one escapes their destiny.

The temples of Delphi were destroyed on many occasions by earthquakes and landslides, and rebuilt each time over the ruins. The "Delphi business" was hot property. The Pythia murmured her oracles, sitting upon a tripod above a chasm in the earth, from which steam poured forth. There has been much speculation about this, and recently geologists have even announced the discovery, in the temple area, of geological fault zones, under which there are layers containing hydrocarbon: "Such formations often emit gases such as ethylene's, methane and hydrogen supplied."[29] These gases could, it is said, have induced in the Pythia a "kind of drugged state and stimulated her visions." I don't believe a word of it. No one knows precisely what occurred in the temple of Apollo, although all Greek writers turned their attention to it. The Greek historian Plutarch describes the oracle process "but Plutarch adhered to what was a matter of course for all priests of Apollo: to breathe no word about what happened in the house of the god."[30] Each tourist who clambers up the slope on zigzag paths ought to take a closer look at the foundations of the (often renovated) temple of Apollo. The antiquity of the megaliths oozes from every crack. And the mighty slabs of stone which nowadays cover the ground, and on which columns formerly stood, make one think immediately of a helicopter landing platform. This platform dates back to the 6th century BC. The foundation, the so-called "Polygonal Wall," is older. I recommend everyone to pause for a moment at this spot, to sit down on a step of the Delphi theatre, and let the past come to life before one's inner eye.

Looking outwards from the semicircular amphitheatre all Delphi lies at your feet. (Above on the slope there is another sports arena which dates back to Roman times.) The Delphi below you consists of the ruins of buildings in which people once thronged, amongst them petitioners and people in despair, politicians and delegates, priests, and tradesmen on the look-out for a fast buck. One thing alone united them all: a belief in Apollo and his power. I doubt if they also believed in the oracle, for it seems to have been more a sort of guide or help, rather like our newspaper horoscopes. Each person could take from it what he wanted.

Below, 13 statues of gods and heroes once stood, as well as the treasure houses of the Sicyon's, Siphniens, Thebans, and Athenians. There were statues, marble pillars and the bronze statue of the chariot driver (now in the Delphi museum). And of course we must not forget to mention the 52-foot (16m) high statue of the god Apollo standing before his huge temple. Pausanius writes that the temple of Apollo was probably originally made of metal.

And in the midst of all this, between treasure houses, temples, round buildings, and marble pillars, one notices a very strange, longish stone in the shape of a beehive. Upon it is engraved a confusing network of lines, most of which intersect with other lines at equal intervals. This is the omphalos, symbolizing the navel of the world. An imitation from Roman times nowadays stands in the Delphi museum. The original omphalos had precious stones at the lines' intersection points, and over this egg-shaped stone hung two golden eagles. With this stone carving, Apollo, or the priests, or if you like a petrified mythology, hit the nail on the head—whether intentionally or by chance.

I must recall something which I first suggested in 1979, in my book *Prophet der Veryangenheit* ("Prophet of the Past").[31] In 1974, I gave a lecture in Athens, during which a bald-headed man came to my attention because he was taking copious notes. As everyone left the room he came up to me and inquired politely whether I knew that most Greek shrines and sacred places were sited in an exact geometrical relationship to one another.

I smiled and said that I couldn't really believe that, because the "ancient Greeks" did not have geodesic surveying techniques at their disposal. In addition, I said, the temples were often many miles distant from one another, and the mountains of Greece would have made it impossible to get a direct view from one holy site to another. Lastly, thinking I knew better, I said that the sacred sites were sometimes situated on islands, often as much as 60 miles away from the mainland, and could therefore not be seen with the naked eye. I was thinking of the distances to Crete, or Izmir, previously known as Smyrna, in Turkey. So what could this friendly gentleman mean?

Two days later we met again, this time not on a public occasion but at a lecture given for members of the Athens Rotary Club. After the discussion he invited me into an adjoining room, where land and aerial maps were spread out on a large table. The gentleman introduced himself as Dr. Theophanias Manias, a brigadier in the Greek air force. What did such a high-ranking military fellow have to do with archaeology? We drank tea together and he explained. It was usual, he said, for military pilots to undertake monitoring and practice flights over the mountains, or shooting exercises over the sea. Afterward they had to draft a report, which included, among other things, the amount of fuel used. Through the years it had dawned on a lieutenant who entered these data in a book that the same distances and fuel consumption recurred again and again, although the pilots flew different routes over different regions. The lieutenant thought that he had tracked down some kind of fraud, or that the pilots were perhaps too lazy to write up the correct amounts in their log books and were just copying from each other.

This was investigated, and finally the file landed on the desk of Colonel Manias—he became brigadier later. He took a pair of compasses, placed the point on Delphi and drew a circle through the Acropolis. Strange to say the circumference of the circle also touched Argos and Olympia. These places were equal distances from each other. A strange coincidence, thought Colonel Manias, and then placed the compass point on Knossos at Crete. The circumference of this circle also touched Sparta and Epidaurus—strange! Colonel Manias continued. When the centre was Delos, Thebes and Izmir lay on the circumference; when the centre was Paros, it was Knossos and Chalcis; when the centre was Sparta, Mycenae and the oracular site of Trofonion were on the circumference.

Dr. Manias demonstrated this to me on the maps he had spread out, and I was staggered. How could that be? Although Dr. Manias had far more accurate maps available to him than one can normally buy in the shops, I decided to try this out for myself at home. The brigadier noticed my astonishment and asked me if I had heard of the "golden ratio." I shook my head rather despondently: although I had vague memories of hearing about a "golden ratio" in some long-past geometry lesson, I couldn't remember what it was. Patiently he explained it to me: "In the golden ratio, a distance is divided into two sections, so that the smaller section relates to the larger as the larger does to the whole distance." Because I did not understand a word of all this, I grabbed my daughter's geometry book when I got home and read:

> If a distance A-B is divided by a point E in such a way that the whole distance relates to its larger section as this larger section does to the smaller, then one says that the distance A-B is in "golden ratio." If one increases a distance divided in golden ratio by the length of its larger section, the new distance is once more divided into golden ratio by the endpoint of the original distance. This process can be continued ad infinitum.[32]

I felt sorry for my daughter. This was as comprehensible to me as Chinese! I started to try to work it out on my desk with bits of paper. My secretary Kilian looked on with a rather concerned air as if he feared I was losing my marbles. After fiddling about with larger and smaller sections for a long while, I finally grasped what the golden ratio was all about. I recommend my readers to try the same "hands-on" method. Dr. Manias showed me tables and demonstrated it on his maps, and everyone who checks this out will be bowled over:

- The distance between the cult sites of Epidaurus and Delphi corresponds to the greater portion, that is 62 percent, of the golden ratio distance between Epidaurus and Delos.

- The distance between Olympia and Chalcis corresponds to the greater portion (62 percent) of the golden ratio distance between Olympia and Delos.

- The distance between Delphi and Thebes corresponds to the greater portion (62 percent) of the golden ratio distance between Delphi and the Acropolis.

- The distance between Olympia and Delphi corresponds to the greater portion (62 percent) of the golden ratio distance between Olympia and Chalcis.

- The distance between Epidaurus and Sparta corresponds to the greater portion (62 percent) of the golden ratio distance between Epidaurus and Olympia.

- The distance between Delos and Eleusis corresponds to the greater portion (62 percent) of the golden ratio distance between Delos and Delphi.

- The distance between Knossos and Delos corresponds to the greater portion (62 percent) of the golden ratio distance between Knossos and Chalcis.

- The distance between Delphi and Dodoni corresponds to the greater portion (62 percent) of the golden ratio distance between Delphi and the Acropolis.

- The distance between Sparta and Olympia corresponds to the greater portion (62 percent) of the golden ratio distance between Sparta and the Acropolis.

I was knocked sideways! Dr. Manias informed me that there existed in Greece an Association for Operational Research whose very educated members had held lectures about these geometrical curiosities, for example on June 18, 1968, in the premises of the Greek Technical Association, as well as at the headquarters of the Greek air force. The audiences had been as baffled as I had been. I later got hold of a document in two languages put out by the Association for Operational Research, which had been written with the active support of the Military Geography Department.[33, 34] Dr. Manias also gave me a handsome brochure, which documents all these mathematical impossibilities in a way which even a layman like myself can check.[35] Dr. Manias expressly asked me to draw attention to these geometrical aspects for, as he said, the archaeologists behaved as if they did not exist.

They do exist—and how! The conclusions to be drawn from these geometrical facts, which cannot be ignored, and which everyone can measure for themselves, are fantastic. But first a few appetizers:

- How great is the probability that three temples in mountain regions lie on a straight line by pure coincidence? That might perhaps occur in two or three cases. But in Attica-Boetia (central Greece) alone, there are 35 of these "three-temple lines." This rules out mere chance.

- What chance is there that the distance from one holy site to another is the same in several instances (measured as the crow flies)? In central Greece this occurs 22 times!

- And Delphi, the "navel of the world," occupies a position within this network equivalent to a central airport. Either starting from Delphi, or involving it, the most incredible geodesic measurements arise. For example Delphi is equidistant from the Acropolis and Olympia. One can draw a perfect isosceles triangle. At the midpoint of the "leg" (one of the two shorter sides of a right-angled triangle) lies the holy site of Nemea. The right-angled triangles Acropolis-Delphi—Nemea, and Nemea-Delphi—Olympia, have hypotenuses of equal length, and their relationship to the common line Delphi-Nemea corresponds to the golden ratio. You may think this is confusing enough, but it gets worse!

A line drawn through Delphi which is vertical to the Delphi-Olympia horizontal crosses the oracle site of Dodoni. This produces the right-angled triangle Delphi-Olympia-Dodoni, with the line between Dodoni and Olympia as the hypotenuse. The "legs" of this triangle are once more in golden ratio proportions.

What on earth is going on? You may think it is all artificially imposed, but there is method in this madness. The distance from Delphi to Aphea is the same as the distance from Aphea to Sparta. The distance from Delphi to Sparta is the same as the distance from Sparta to Thebes, and by chance also half the distance of the Dodoni-Sparta and Dodoni-Acropolis lines. Equal distances also apply to lines drawn between Delphi and Mycenae, Mycenae and Athens, Delphi and Gortys (a megalithic ruin on Crete!), and Delphi and Milet in Asia Minor. To sum up we can see that Delphi stands in geodesic/geometric relationship to Olympia, Dodoni, Eleusis, Epidaurus, Aphea, the Acropolis, Sparta, Mycenae, Thebes, Chalcis, Nemea, Gortys, and Milet. I would like to thank Dr. Manias and the Association for Operational Research for pointing out these extraordinary relationships. But that is still not the whole story.

Everyone can picture an isosceles triangle, and such triangles joining cult sites cannot just arise by chance. Someone must have had an overview. In ancient Greece many such triangles can be drawn, and always with two proportions in regard to the length of their sides. For example:

- The Dodoni-Delphi-Sparta triangle: The distances between these places are in the same relationship to one another as Dodoni-Sparta to Dodoni-Delphi, Dodoni-Sparta to Sparta-Delphi, and Dodoni-Delphi to Delphi-Sparta.

- The Knossos-Delos-Chalcis triangle: The distances between these places are in the same relationship to one another as Knossos-Chalcis to Knossos-Delos, Knossos-Chalcis to Chalcis-Delos, and Knossos-Delos to Delos-Chalcis.

- The Nicosia (Cyprus)-Knossos (Crete)-Dodoni triangle: The distances between these places are in the same relationship to one another as Nicosia-Dodon to Nicosia-Knossos, Nicosia-Dodoni to Dodoni-Knossos, and Nicosia-Knossos to Knossos-Dodoni.

All these triangles are the same. There are more such baffling examples, but I would prefer not to overwhelm my readers with geometry.

Using maps on a scale of 1:10,000 and with help of the Military Geography Department, the Association for Operational Research discovered more than 200 equal geometrical relationships, resulting from the same number of isosceles triangles. In addition they found 148 golden ratio proportions. Anyone who still speaks of coincidence needs his head examined. Of course, one can always join two places by drawing a random line, and discover that other places lie on the same line "by chance." However, we are not talking of any old names on a map, but exclusively of ancient, or, to be more precise, prehistoric cult sites. The planning which underlies this phenomenon is incomprehensible. Unless of course the network was not planned as such, but arose from a quite different, compelling reason. But before we come to that, we need to draw breath for a moment.

Professor Fritz Rogowski, of Braunschweig Technical College, told himself that it was quite easy to construct right-angled triangles in the landscape, and set off to prove it. In Greece's mountainous terrain he found small stone circles here and there, then looked around for additional markings; and lo and behold, in many cases he discovered a second stone ring within his field of vision.[36] Professor Rogowski then extended the line of these two marking points, and at the end of such a sequence occasionally found a cult site. So had the riddle been solved?

No, it hadn't. Too many of the lines joining ancient cult sites pass over the sea. A line of the Delphi-Olympia-Acropolis triangle bridges about 12.5 miles (20km) of sea. The same is true for the Dodoni-Sparta line. It becomes even more absurd with triangles such as Knossos-Delos-Argos, for Knossos on Crete and Argos are separated by about 190 miles (300km) of sea.[37] This small-scale surveying method would have been just as impossible when applied to the stretch of sea between Greece and Smyrna. I also seriously doubt whether this surveying technique even works on dry land. There would be no problem if we were dealing with a flat and even landscape, but there certainly is a problem in mountainous terrain and in a landscape carved by countless bays and inlets, such as Greece supplies. So what purpose did the small stone rings serve which Professor Rogowski found? I could imagine that they might be signs to help travellers find their bearings. After all, there were no roads as such in prehistoric times, and tracks and paths might soon be washed away by storms and floods.

The clever scholars of today hold fast to the principle of the "simplest possibility," of the solution that is "nearest to hand." But this blinds them to any other perspective. They are imprisoned in their habits of thought, for they take the answer nearest to hand to be the one and only solution. So why study any further? This method, even if it is given the holy stamp of scientific approval, offers only half-solutions to deeper questions. One of these non-solutions, which lulls science into happy slumbers, is derived from knowledge which the ancient Greek mathematicians had—Euclid, for example, who lived in the 4th and 3rd centuries BC, and who gave dissertations in Egypt and Greece. He wrote several textbooks which dealt not only with the whole spectrum of mathematics but also all of geometry including proportions, or confusing subjects such as "quadratic irrationality" and "stereometry." Euclid was a contemporary of the philosopher Plato, who in turn occasionally got involved in politics. Plato is said to have sat at Euclid's feet and listened to his dissertations on geometry. So it may be tempting to believe that Plato was so enthused by the mathematical genius Euclid that he decided to turn this knowledge to practical use, in building projects which he, as a politician, might have a hand in organizing. So what did Plato know?

In the dialogue *The Republic*, Plato tells his conversation partners that area is part of geometry. In another dialogue (*Menon* or "On Virtue"), he even enters into discussion with a slave, and uses the fellow's lack of knowledge to demonstrate higher geometry. But it is in the dialogue *Timaeus* that things really start coming thick and fast, where the problem of proportions, of the product and square numbers is mentioned, as well as what we call the "golden ratio." The following quote may be incomprehensible to people like me who never managed to follow higher mathematics. But it shows the high level of mathematical discussion that went on more than 2,500 years ago:

> For when out of three numbers, whether products or square numbers, the middle one relates to the last as the first to the middle,

and equally the last to the middle as the middle to the first, it then comes about that if one moves the middle to the first and last position, and places the first and last instead in the middle, the relationship always remains the same. But if they always remain in the same relationship to one another, they form a unity together. Thus if the earth were to have become a simple surface without depth, then a middle realm would have sufficed for it to unite itself with the two other realms.[38]

This goes on until one's head is splitting. After plowing through the following horrendous sentence I gave up all desire to follow Plato's mathematical explanations:

But since new gaps of 3/2, 4/3 and 9/8 arose within the original gaps through this unification, all gaps of 4/3 were filled by the gap of 9/8, and thus left in each a small part over as further gap, whose limits relate to one another in the ratio of 256 to 243.[39]

What is the subject of this complicated Platonic dialogue? The creation of the Earth. After spending a few weeks in Plato's company, I no longer understood why Galileo Galilei caused such a stir with his "new" doctrine, and why the Christian Inquisition wished to kill him in the 17th century. Everything which Galileo taught was already there in Plato—such as the fact that the Earth is a globe, or that our planet orbits the sun. Yet all this, including the laws of gravity, was dealt with in ancient Indian texts even longer ago. It seems that the ancients knew an awful lot more than our secondary school pupils are told. Gaius Plinius Caecilius Secundus (AD 61–113), who must have studied Plato and Euclid, gives us this impressive demonstration of the knowledge he got from them:

There is a great dispute amongst the scholars and the common people about whether the earth is inhabited by people whose feet [on opposite sides of the globe] are turned towards each other. The latter ask why it is that the "opposite-footed" don't fall. As if the "opposite-footed" ones might not ask exactly the same question about us.... It does however seem miraculous that the earth forms a globe, with all the vast surfaces of the oceans.... This is why it is never day and night at the same time all over the earth, for night comes to the side opposite to that on which the sun shines.[40]

Nothing new under the sun! So does the geometric network linking the Greek temples come from Plato or his predecessor Euclid? Were the holy places only allowed to be built at geometrically determined points? If so, where did these points come from? Where did this geometry itself come from? Why these proportional relationships? Why the golden ratio?

Plato, Callicles, Chairephon, Gorgias, and Socrates all took part in the Gorgias dialogue—a truly intellectual bunch. First of all, Socrates emphasizes that what he has to say is his own conviction, the truth of which he can vouch for. Then he declares that geometrical wisdom is not just important among human beings, but played an important role for the gods too. But how does such knowledge get passed on from the gods to man? This is explained in the third book of Plato's *Laws*. The participants speak, once again, about civilizations of the past. An Athenian asks Plato whether he believes he knows how much time has passed since there were first nations and people on the Earth.

Then the question is thrown up as to whether there may be a core of truth in the old legends. Already then! They were speaking expressly of those legends "of former numerous catastrophes which overcame mankind, through floods and other disasters, from which only a tiny proportion of humanity was preserved."[41] They talk about how only inhabitants of mountain regions survived, who after only a few generations had lost all memory of earlier civilizations. People considered what was "said about the gods as simply true, and lived their lives accordingly." To regulate their lives after the flood, Plato said, they had to develop new rules and laws, because none of the lawgivers of former times had survived. Here is a quote from Plato's *Laws* (my emphasis added): "But since we do not give laws for the sons of gods and heroes, as the lawgivers of former times, *who themselves descended from gods*, gave laws...no one will be able to hold it against us."[42]

The gods admired by the Greeks themselves descended from other gods, from whom the original laws had been handed down. So did offspring of the gods also give orders for a geometrical arrangement of temples? Rubbish! Why should they? And Plato, Socrates, and Euclid have nothing to do with it either.

Professor Neugebauer compares Platonic geometry with that of Euclid, and with geometry from Assur and Egypt. He finds little in Plato that couldn't be found elsewhere.[43] And Professor Jean Richter discovers in the temple arrangements of ancient Greece a geometry which existed long before Euclid.[44] Only the question as to why there might be a need for such geometrical arrangements remains unanswered. These professorial discoveries really do make all further questions redundant. The answer "nearest to hand" on this occasion does for once make other possible answers just so much time-wasting. Let me put it quite clearly: The ancient Greek mathematicians cannot have had anything to do with the geometrical arrangement of sacred sites, because these places were already regarded as sacred millennia before these mathematicians were born. Neither Euclid, nor Plato, nor Socrates had a hand in it. The mathematical knowledge of educated Greeks was astonishing, but they did not ever give orders, whether political or of any other kind, to say where a temple should be constructed—for these temples had already stood where they were for long ages of time. So how—and now we come to the central question—did the clear geometrical network over all of Greece come about?

Fairy tales begin with "Once upon a time...." I would like to start slightly differently: "Let's just assume...." that at some distant time extraterrestrials visited our earth. These were the ur-gods. They managed to produce children: the Titans and giants who wandered the earth. These were slaughtered and new gods created—such mythological figures as Apollo, Perseus, Poseidon, and Athene. These divided the earth amongst themselves and again started to produce offspring.

The umpteenth generation of these gods was still able to impress slow-witted humans with their technical achievements. They possessed superior weapons and, in particular, they could fly! It is true that their machines were no longer much more than rattling, stinking, flying monsters, but they did propel themselves through the air after a fashion, and that was enough to impress their admiring subjects. Whoever can raise himself into the air must be divine! However, these flying tubs needed fuel, even if this was only a bit of oil, charcoal, or water for the steam engine. Their pilots knew exactly how far they could fly before they needed to refuel. It is possible that there were different types of flying vessels, for longer or shorter trips (at least this is said of the flying vehicles in ancient India).

It was very convenient for the gods that human beings set up sacred places in their honor, for it was at such places that they could collect the "offerings"; and the "mortals" were also reverent enough to serve the "immortals" in whatever way they could. The whole world thus became Shangri-La for them. It was quite logical that sacred sites always occurred at the same intervals, for after a certain number of miles the flying contraptions needed to refuel. And once the grandiose sites of offerings to the gods—or perhaps one should say their self-service stations—were there, they stayed where they were.

The families of the gods and a few close friends were also told the positions of these self-service stations: if you fly from Delphi at an angle of X, for 40 miles, you will come to Y. Fly on for 40 miles in a straight line and you will come to Z. Nothing simpler. The geometrical network thus arises quite naturally from their "refueling points" or "service stations." And naturally the distances are all the same, since new supplies must be taken on after a certain number of miles. After all, none of the gods should get lost on the journey, no family member should come to harm because a distance was too great and the flying machine ran out of fuel suddenly.

I began this section with an assumption, no more than that. I know of no other assumption which can solve the riddle of the geometrical network in Greece more simply and elegantly. The only proviso is that one subscribes to the idea that "descendants of the gods" once really walked the earth. And if one knows how to look, one can find any quantity of ancient tales to support this.

Even when the gods' families had long since become degenerate, certain of these parasites still seem to have managed to exploit human beings' lack of knowledge. In his first book, Herodotus describes the city of Babylon, giving precise details of its size and such things. In the center, he says, there once stood a temple to Zeus (Belos), "with iron doors which were still there in my own day." This had eight towers, built one upon the other. The entrance to this high tower was a stairway which spiraled around the outside of all the towers.

On the topmost tower there was a "great temple, and within it a broad bed with lovely canopies, and next to it a golden table." No one was allowed to enter there, except for a very beautiful woman who had been chosen. This was, the priests told Herodotus, because the god personally enters the temple and sleeps in the bed, "and something similar occurs, according to Egyptian teachings, in Egyptian Thebes. There too a woman sleeps within the temple of Zeus at Thebes. It is said that these women never have intercourse with mortal men. The same is true of the priestess of the god in Patara in Lycia, when the god appears. When he appears the woman is enclosed with him in the temple at night."

Exactly the same thing happened in the high towers of Indian temples. And it was for the same reason that the peoples of Central America built their step pyramids, with a room at the apex. It is quite clear why towers and pyramids were needed: the fellows arrived by air!

In Herodotus' time, the gods' families no longer existed, for otherwise he would have written about their flying ships. But in former times things had been just as the Babylonian priests told him. The gods took their pleasure with women and men, here, there, and everywhere. When the gods started to arrive less and less frequently, and eventually stopped coming altogether, the sly priests turned the whole Shangri-La to their own advantage. It was now they to whom offerings should be made, they to whom maidens and youths should be brought and to whom gold and diamonds were to be delivered. A few generations down the line the priests no longer knew how the whole thing had started—but why give up such a lucrative business?

But even the high priest was plagued by a daily uncertainty. He knew of the power of the gods from tradition, even if he understood nothing about it. And he did not know when a god might return. Wasn't it therefore more sensible to exploit people only to the extent that was necessary to retain his own power? And hoard treasure to offer the gods on their return? That would surely appease these heavenly and incomprehensible beings, wouldn't it?

But all these assumptions presuppose that there were flying wagons in antiquity in the first place. That can be shown to have been the case, certainly in the ancient literature.

The Indian King Rumanvat, who reigned thousands of years ago, had a "celestial ship" built in which several groups of people could be transported at once.[45] There are more than 50 passages in the Indian epics *Ramayana* and *Mahabharata* which explicitly deal with flying machines,[46] and the Ethiopian *Book of Kings* describes King Solomon's flying wagon even indicating the speeds at which it flew.[47] I have already dealt briefly with Solomon's flights a few pages earlier. We know about his flights to the Queen of Sheba in what is now Yemen. But Solomon's love life is more complex than that. Allow me briefly to explain:

The official title of the Ethiopian *Book of Kings* is called *Kebra Negest*. Its origins are unknown, but this large work was translated from Ethiopian into Arabic in AD 409. Right at the beginning it reports about the love affair between "Makeda," the Queen of Ethiopia, and the Israelite King Solomon. Solomon, who claimed a monopoly on wisdom, was an insatiable playboy, according to these reports, who certainly did not restrict himself to the women in his home country in taking his pleasures. He also fetched ladies from beyond his borders. The Ethiopian queen, in turn, had heard of Solomon, including that he was rich and very handsome. So she prepared an expedition to Jerusalem. She had 797 camels saddled and numerous donkeys laden. She set up camp before the walls of Jerusalem and Solomon was so smitten by her grace and beauty that he had rich gifts sent to her:

> He honored her and gave her habitation in a royal palace very close by. He sent her food for the evening and morning meal, and each day fifteen kor (an ancient Hebrew unit of measure) of finely ground wheatmeal with a great quantity of oil, from which bread

for 350 people was prepared. Also accessories of porcelain platters, 10 fattened oxen and 50 sheep. Then wine, and each day eleven dazzling garments.[48]

The gifts did their work and Solomon comprehensively seduced the beautiful queen. At her departure he also splashed out: "He made her gifts of all desirable glories and riches, dazzlingly beautiful garments and all the glories desired by the country of Ethiopia. Including a wagon that flew through the air...."[49]

The chronicler of the *Kebra Negest* clearly differentiates between vehicles with wheels which move across land and *a wagon that flew through the air*. Solomon wanted his lover to visit him often without always having to organize elaborate expeditions on each occasion. Nine months and five days after their first meeting, the queen gave birth to a boy whom she called Baina-lehkem. When this prince turned 22 years of age, he visited his father in Jerusalem for the first time. But the boy did not just want to get to know Solomon, he wanted more: the holy Ark of the Covenant of the Israelites. This was one wish which Solomon could not fulfill for his son. It was unthinkable that the Ark of the Covenant, which Moses had received from his God, should be given as a gift to the Ethiopians.

But the royal scion was clever. He had a perfect replica of the Ark made. One night he made the priests in the Tabernacle of the Temple drunk and stole the real Ark of the Covenant. He had the copy put in its place and the Israelites did not noticed the sacrilege until it was already too late. Because Baina-lehkem *flew* with his prize to Ethiopia:

> the wagon flew through the air and all the people and animals who were on the wagon were lifted up...and all sped along on the flying wagon like a ship on the sea, like an eagle as it effortlessly flies on the wind....[50]

Solomon and his warriors pursued the flying wagon but did not stand a chance:

> And the inhabitants of the land of Egypt told them: the people from Ethiopia came past here, driving on a wagon like the angels, and

they were faster than an eagle in the heavens. The inhabitants of the cities bore witness...that those from Ethiopia flew, and that the statues of the gods fell over and smashed, and the obelisks were also destroyed....[51]

An extraordinary flying machine which even made statutes of the gods and obelisks fall over? And why were Solomon's fast riders unable to catch up with Baina-lehkem? The *Kebra Negest* provides the answer: They flew on the wagon without sickness and suffering, without hunger and thirst, without sweat and exhaustion, covering a distance of three months in one day.[52]

That is no mean feat. If we assume that a distance of 40 kilometers can be covered in a day, then this corresponds to 3,600 kilometers in three months. This distance was covered by the flying wagon in one day. Perplexing. As I already described, the *Kebra Negest* also mentions visits of King Solomon to the Queen of Sheba in what is Yemen today, whereby the boundaries between the Queen of Ethiopia and the Queen of Sheba are fluid. Possibly the same lover was meant.

There is literary proof of prehistoric air travel, but no remains of these flying craft have ever been found. That is not surprising. By comparison, the end of last World War is only just 65 years in the past and all the nations involved must have deployed thousands of aircraft in total. Where are their remains today? Other than in museums, there is nothing left. Nature does not just turn temples into ruins—it also makes the technology of antiquity crumble to dust.

I have demonstrated the geometric grid that covered the whole of ancient Greece. I suggested that flying craft are responsible for the recurring equal distances because their restricted technology simply did not allow any longer flights. The gods and their descendants were forced to make "pit stops." There is another possible solution for the geometric grid which covers Greece.

I will assume that my general hypothesis is familiar: many thousands of years ago, aliens visited the earth. But they did not just push off without as much as a by-your-leave without leaving some evidence of their existence. Let us assume that evidence was a kind of "time capsule," indestructible for millennia. Inside, it would have to say, "We were here... from that galaxy...using this or that technology...we found intelligent life here...we instructed them...we continued on our travels...we will return in x-thousand years..." Wherever they hid this capsule, the space travelers of thousands of years ago would *additionally* have had to ensure that it would even occur to the human beings in the far distant future to look for it. How do you get people thousands of years in the future to do something of which they have no idea?

You leave such obvious hints that the human beings of the future cannot but notice them. The Stone Age types in ancient Greece considered the extraterrestrials to be gods. We know today that there are no gods—but our far distant ancestors did not have that understanding. Those people wished to worship the gods, build monuments to them, so that their descendants would also always remember the gods. Okay, said the "gods," but you will build your holy places precisely where we tell you to. In this way the geometric pattern over Greece was created with always identical distances between one place and another and the recurring angles. What was the point of that for the "gods"? They knew that the human beings of the future would themselves fly one day, that they would survey and catalogue their planet. Sooner or later it had to come to the attention of the people of the future that there was something odd about the sacred sites in ancient Greece. They would invariably come across the geometric pattern and notice that it could never have been planned by Stone Age people. They lacked the surveying instruments for that. After all, Greece is a mountainous country with a broken coastline. Many distances, such as from Delphi to Crete, for example, were not visible to the naked eye. There *had* to be planning behind it. But by whom?

As a consequence, all kinds of questions would be asked. Including the question: did our ancestors have visitors from space? Were extraterrestrials the teachers of the young Greeks? There would be the usual counter arguments which at some point would culminate in the question: if there were ETs—where's the evidence? The extraterrestrials did not, after all, just push off without leaving some objective evidence.

At that point the geometric grid over Greece would have fulfilled its purpose. And that is precisely the point at which humanity stands today. Now the following question should be considered with cool scientific reason: by what pattern should we proceed to find the millennia-old time capsule of those "gods"?

We are in the third millennium. Gods went a long time ago. But their legacy still exists. The time has come to look for these precious messages.

Chapter 4
The Trojan Tangle

If the sun rises in the West, put your compass to the test!

—Folk saying

At the end of the 8th century BC in Greece, there lived a poet whose name is now known all over the world, yet about whom no one knows anything for certain: Homer (Homeros in Greek), author of the fantastic epics the *Iliad* and the *Odyssey*. Research has shown that Homer was a native of Asia Minor, and was probably a wandering singer or minstrel. He is also said to have been blind. What remains a mystery is where this blind minstrel got the framework for his stories, the "inside information" for his ambitious tales. The *Iliad* and *Odyssey* consist of 28,000 verses—not bad for a blind poet. Greek poetry is considered to have begun with Homer; he stands "at the beginning of Greek literature, and with him begins the history of the European mind."[1]

Even Homer did not simply fabricate his tales out of nothing. Experts believe that the written versions of his epics followed a long oral tradition, and that at its core a "very ancient folktale tradition" is hidden.[2]

And what is the subject of this "very ancient folktale"?

In the *Iliad* are described battles, curious weapons and the deeds of heroes, in which both gods and men participate. We read in the eighth canto of "flying horses" which fly back and forth "between the earth and the star-strewn heavens." These divine beasts remain invisible, thanks to a mist or fog. The ruler of the sea, Poseidon, is transported over the water by a team of flying horses, so that not even the axle of his chariot touches the waves. I'm rather partial to such fairy tales. Of course the whole thing has to do with love, offended honor, and—to a lesser extent—with the Trojan War itself.

Things are different in the *Odyssey*. Here we read of the hair-raising adventures of Odysseus. With his fellow warriors, he finally conquers Troy and, after 20 years, eventually returns to his homeland of Ithaca. The whole epic revolves around Odysseus himself: he tells the story in the first person, of the blows of fate which the gods have seen fit to aim at him, but also of his own heroic deeds and tricks which enable him to survive. Philologists regard Odysseus as an "ancient figure of legend."[3] And the whole story is of course "in the nature of a fable."[4] For a long time, no one thought that it could be based on actual events—until Heinrich Schliemann (1822–90), with Homer in his hand, discovered the city of Troy. But we will return to that.

I don't wish to analyze the *Odyssey* as I did the *Argonautica*. There is enough written about it already. But I must give a few points of reference for understanding this earth-shaking story.

Odysseus (in Latin Ulysses or Ulixes) is the king of Ithaca. He and his companions set off to conquer Troy, because the beautiful Helen of Sparta had been "abducted" and taken there. On the way home, Odysseus' fleet, which starts out as 12 ships, meets one adventure after another. First the heroes are blown onto Cape Malea, then they land on the island of the one-eyed Cyclops. One of these, Polyphemus, imprisons Odysseus and his companions in his cave, and eats two of them each day. Finally, Odysseus manages to blind the Cyclops' eye with a red-hot stake and to escape with the rest of his crew. (It should be mentioned in passing that the Cyclops asks Odysseus his name, and that he lies, saying his name is "No one." After he is blinded, Polyphemus calls his fellow Cyclops to help him, and cries out "No one has done this to me.")

Odysseus and his crew then have to deal with the allure of the Sirens and with the lady magician Circe, who turns the whole crew into pigs. After this Odysseus visits the realm of Hades—the underworld of the dead— where he may speak not only with his dead mother but also with other famous figures who have long since departed this life. Finally the ship has to pass between two female terrors, Scylla and Charybdis. Charybdis is said to have once been hurled into the sea by a bolt of Zeus' lightning, and since then, three times a day, she sucks down huge amounts of water and spits it out again. Her sister Scylla is no less daunting. She is described as a dog-like monster who grabs passing sailors and slowly eats them. She snatches six of Odysseus' men straight away.

The remaining crew reach the island of Trinacria, and, because they are hungry, slaughter some cows. Unfortunately, though, the beasts belong to the Sun-Titan Hyperion, who complains furiously to Odysseus and then blasts both ship and crew to smithereens with a single lightning bolt. Only Odysseus survives. He grasps hold of a few planks and is washed up some days later on the island of Ogygia, which belongs to Calypso, who, in spite of her beauty, dwells in a cave. She pampers and spoils Odysseus and begs him to remain with her, offering him immortality in return.

For seven years Odysseus enjoys the good life, but finally has enough of being endlessly kissed and feted. Sadly he sits on the shore and dreams of his homeland. Then Hermes flies by and orders Calypso to release Odysseus. He is given the tools necessary to build a raft, and sails away on it from Calypso's love-nest. But the sea-god Poseidon, whose son, the Cyclops, had been tricked by Odysseus, tears over the waters on his winged chariot and knocks Odysseus overboard. If he hadn't managed to pull off his heavy clothes under water he would have drowned.

Two days later he is thrown up, exhausted, on the shores of the island of Drepane. After a short stay with a swineherd, and with the help of divine intervention, he finally reaches Ithaca after an absence of 20 years.

This is the broad outline of the epic. Because there are many geographical details in the *Odyssey* and the Iliad, just as there were in the *Argonautica*, scholars asked themselves where Odysseus had journeyed.

In which sea did his adventures take place? Where are the islands that are mentioned? Where are the dreadful dangers of Scylla and Charybdis located? More than 100 different opinions were expressed, and about 70 maps drawn, and each researcher was sure that he had traced Odysseus' journey correctly. Depending on which version you choose, Odysseus circumnavigated Asia Minor, sailed round the British Isles, or even went as far as South America. It has also been suggested that the *Odyssey* and the *Argonautica* were one and the same journey, or that Odysseus' wanderings took place somewhere other than on Earth.

The most sensible suggestion comes from the German brothers Hans-Helmut and Armin Wolf. They succeed in reconstructing a route in which the time taken on the journey corresponds to places along the way. The authors, however, do not claim that "the Odysseus of legend visited this or that place,"[5] but only that the sea journey which Homer describes can be clearly related to a route through the Mediterranean. Although the result of their long years of research is certainly consistent and convincing, I wonder how the blind Homer could have known the route with such accuracy.

In the *Odyssey*, the island of Crete is also mentioned by name, though without any reference to the robot Talos. Did Homer know the Talos from the *Argonautica* or not? Or did the robot seem too far-fetched to him? I can hardly believe that, given the other "fantasies" which appear in the *Odyssey*. Homer attributes all imaginable kinds of magic arts to the gods, including Poseidon's flying chariot, but there is no mention of the Golden Fleece. In spite of all the hocus pocus which the gods indulge in, the *Odyssey* does not contain any science fiction in *Argonautica* style.

Troy is at the center of the war described in the *Iliad,* and the one place which does not form part of the geometrical network of ancient Greece. Was it not included in the ancient routes of the gods? However, the fate of Troy is described by all ancient Greek historians, and the siege is meant to have occurred between 1194 and 1184 BC. Troy must be very ancient, for the city's name is derived from that of the mythical hero "Tros" (father of Ilos, grandfather of Laomedon, great grandfather of Priam of Troy). Originally the city had other names: Ilium, Ilion, and Troas. Apollo was also said to have helped in building its Cyclopic defenses. Troy therefore has just as "mythic" an origin as the many other sacred centers in Greece that we have already mentioned. So why did the geographical position of the excavation site which is nowadays thought to be Troy not correspond with the geometrical network of the gods? Is the Troy which Heinrich Schliemann discovered not the same as the Troy of mythology?

Agamemnon also figures in the *Odyssey*, and is said to be buried with several of his companions in Mycenae which, unlike "Troy," is part of the geometrical network. This gives me some pause for thought.

According to legend, the region around Troy was once ruled by a Cretan king called Teucros. His people were the Teucrians. But then the lonely king's son Dardanos arrived and founded a small settlement.

The region was soon called Dardania (the Dardanelles) after him, and because his son was called Tros, the settlement was also named Troas or Troy. Because Tros' eldest son bore the name Ilos, the citadel on the hill was also called Ilion or Ilios, which gave rise to the name of Homer's poem the *Iliad*.

Modern legend has it that Heinrich Schliemann came with the *Iliad* in his hand to rediscover this ancient city. Of course, I'm fond of tales like that: someone claims, against all expert opinion, that Homer's battle of Troy really took place, and that its heroes were real. And then he actually finds Troy too. Great! Unfortunately this story is not quite correct.

Heinrich Schliemann was born on January 6, 1822, in Neu-Bukov (Mecklenburg), the son of a poor minister. By the age of 10, he is said to have written an essay in Latin about the Trojan War. In 1836, he began a business apprenticeship, and five years later he sailed for South America as a cabin-boy on the small brig *Dorothma*. The ship was wrecked and the survivors were taken by lifeboat to the coast of Holland.

In Amsterdam, Heinrich Schliemann became a clerk, on an annual salary of 15 dollars. He was regarded as being very careful with money, extremely hard-working, and with an outstanding memory. Once he had mastered Dutch, he turned his attention to English and French. Later he learned other languages, including Russian and Greek. By the age of 25, Schliemann had become a financially independent business agent, and in 1847 founded his own firm in St. Petersburg. In Russia, he achieved great success with the sale of indigo, sulphur, lead, and saltpeter, assuring himself a secure income after only a few years. By chance he was on a business trip to California on July 4, 1850, and thus "automatically" became an

American citizen (for on this date of its founding, the new United States gave citizenship to all who happened to be on its territory).

From 1858 onward, Schliemann made regular trips around the globe. Enamored of his Homer and absolutely convinced that the Troy described in the *Iliad* and the *Odyssey* must once really have existed, he made Athens his home in 1868.

Because he didn't want to bring his Russian wife to Greece, he got divorced and advertised in the paper for a native partner, finding one in the shape of a lovely 19-year-old girl. Faithful to Homer, he christened his first child Agamemnon. Schliemann, who by now had more than 10 million marks in capital, continued his travels until...well, until he found Troy. But this discovery was by no means as straightforward as we are led to believe by popular biographies.

Just over 2 miles (4 km) from the Dardanelles, on territory which today belongs to Turkey, stands the hill of Hissarlik, no more than 4 miles (7 km) from the Aegean coast. The hill has strategic importance, for every ship that wishes to enter the Dardanelles region must pass it first. The ancient Greeks called this place the "Hellespont," because it was the spot where the daughter of King Athamas, Helle, plunged from the Golden Fleece into the sea. Both the Greeks and later the Romans suspected that Homer's Troy was somewhere near here, and perhaps under the hill of Hissarlik. Just over 2 miles (4 km) south of this hill lies the village of Bunarbaschi, and this is where experts of the last century searched for Troy. The inhabitants, however, claimed before Schliemann arrived that these experts were on the wrong track, and that Troy lay beneath the hill of Hissarlik. It was this very controversy that caused the Anglo-American Frank Calvet, who worked as a consular agent both in Athens and Istanbul, to buy the rights to Hissarlik. Frank Calvet was there before Schliemann, and also started excavating before him, in an amateur kind of way. He hoped to persuade the directors of the British Museum in London to back a bigger excavation, but they refused.

In Athens, Schliemann heard of Calvet's intentions, and set off to buy the hill of Hissarlik. The millionaire Schliemann met up with the

ODYSSEY OF THE GODS

Metallic plates like this one found in Cuenca, Ecuador,
are thousands of years old.

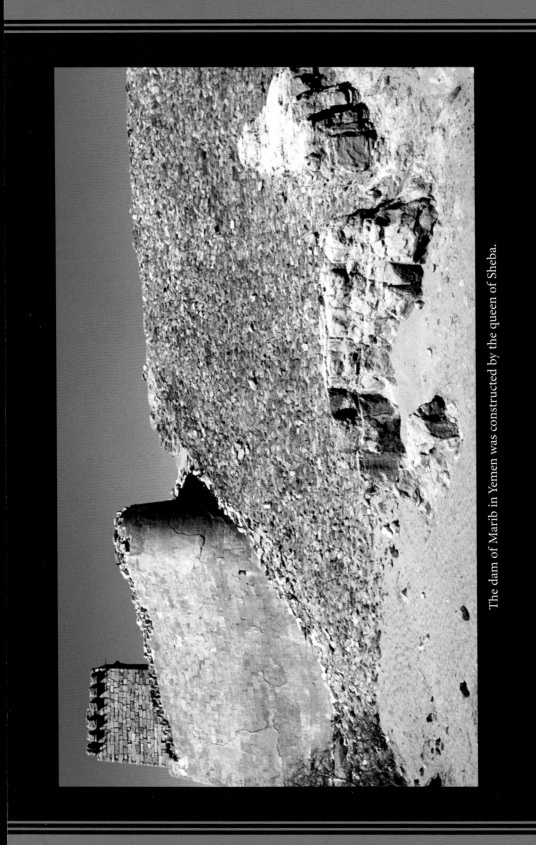

The dam of Marib in Yemen was constructed by the queen of Sheba.

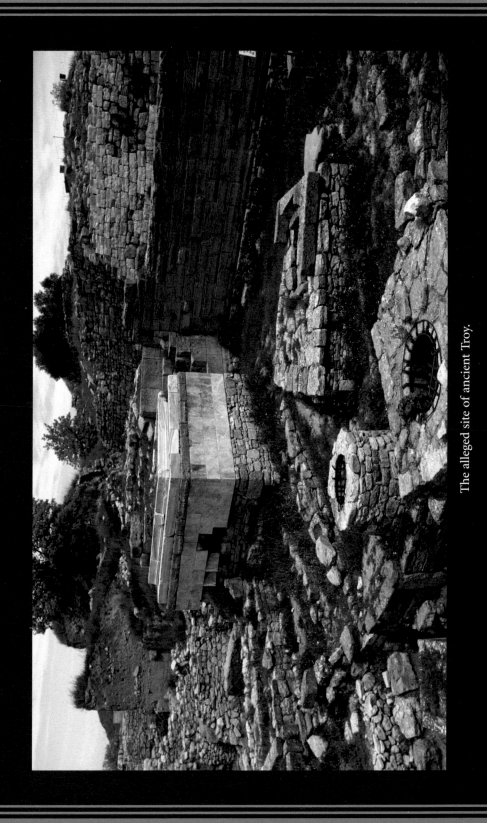

The alleged site of ancient Troy.

The foundations of the Apollo Temple at Delphi.

The ruins of the small temple of the goddess Athena in Delphi.

This sculpture, or *stele*, from Copan, depicts a god. What is he holding in his hands? Is the cross-shaped object between his legs meant to represent some kind of flying belt? The rocket belts of today look similar.

This image from Olympia shows the megalithic part of the stones.

The Machine of Anticythera can be seen at the Greek National Museum in Athens.

The entrance (*above*) and dome (*below*) of the "Treasure House of Atreus" at Mycenae. No one knows what was once stored there.

The Piri Reis map: At the lower edge one can see the ice-free outline of Antarctica, with outlying islands.

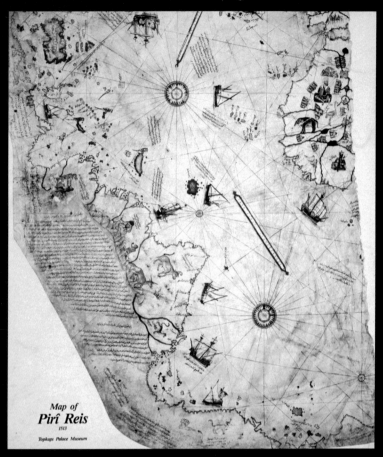

On the island of Malta these rail-like tracks run everywhere. Some of them vanish into the depths of the Mediterranean.

This anthropomorphic sculpture from Copan is a riddle to this day.
Does it reflect a long-lost, forgotten technology?

The Omphalos, or "Navel of the World": This copy, in the Delphi Museum, comes from Roman times. The original boasted precious stones at the points of intersection.

globetrotter Calvet, and the latter was quite happy to give up Hissarlik, together with all the bother it had caused him. When news of the discovery of gold treasure in Troy emerged later, Calvet no doubt kicked himself. Schliemann was certainly a sharp operator, and this was proved in the following years. He was his own best public relations man.

After making the deal with Frank Calvet, several months passed before Schliemann got permission from the Turkish government to start digging at Hissarlik. Finally on October 11, 1871, with a team of 80 workers, the excavations began. Schliemann worked incredibly hard, and even the increasingly cold weather didn't hold him back. He lived in a block-hut with his wife, who tolerated all the discomfort, even though she found the icy wind very hard to bear.

Not until June 15, 1873, did a digger's spade knock against a copper vessel, one filled with golden and silver objects. Schliemann let his workers take an unaccustomed break, and hid the gold treasure in his wife's headscarf. Inside the block-hut he arranged the find, placed a golden diadem on his wife's head, and telegraphed the whole world to say he had found the "treasure of Priam." Naturally some people got annoyed; the Ottoman government accused him of having stolen articles of value from Turkish soil, and envious opponents claimed that he had buried the gold there himself.

Schliemann surmounted every obstacle with his financial power and powers of persuasion. He dug down through layer after layer, and the question was soon not whether he had found Troy but which Troy he had found. Was it Homer's Troy?

He smuggled the supposed "treasure of Priam" out of the country and donated it to the museum of "pre- and early history" in Berlin. The Russians took it from there to the USSR in 1945 as war booty, and claimed to know nothing about it for decades. Since 1993, the Russians and Germans have been in discussion about the treasure, as has the Turkish government, which would like to open a museum containing the finds at the present tourist site of Troy.

Did Schliemann really find the mythical site of Troy, that city which Homer spoke of in the *Iliad* and the *Odyssey*? No one is quite sure. Homer's Troy must have been a mighty city, a place full of educated people, where people knew how to read and write, and where there were temples to the different gods.

Archaeologists have dug their way through 48 layers and found nine different "Troys"—but nowhere did they come across even the smallest tablet bearing the city's name. The only text that was discovered there is engraved with a few Hittite hieroglyphs. It is therefore assumed that Troy was not an "early Greek city, but belonged to a different cultural milieu"[6] that is a Hittite one. This would also explain why Troy was not part of the geometric network of the Greek gods.

Schliemann, however, found nothing but confirmation of his belief. As a gateway was freed from the rubble, he immediately said this was the gateway mentioned by Homer, when he describes how Achilles (of the famous "heel") chases his opponent Hector three times round the city walls. The foundations of a larger building were for Schliemann the "palace of Priam." And in 1872, he thought he had discovered the "high tower" which Homer briefly mentions in the fourth canto of the *Iliad*. Later it turned out that this "tower" was nothing more than two insignificant parallel walls, and that his "palace of Priam" was no larger than a pig-sty. (According to Homer, this palace had 50 bedrooms, halls, and courtyards.) Nor, apparently, could the gateway have been the one mentioned by Homer. In other words, on cooler reflection, Homer's text could not be made to correspond with the interpretation which Schliemann had imposed on many of his finds.

Shortly before he died, Schliemann himself came to doubt whether he had really discovered Homer's Troy. We are still not absolutely certain to this day. His friend and successor in the excavations, the outstanding archaeologist Wilhelm Dorpfeld, pointed out various discrepancies to him. In regard to Mycenae, where Schliemann later dug, he is said to have taken his mistakes with good grace: "What?" he called out once, "isn't this Agamemnon's corpse and treasure after all? Good! Let's call him the mayor instead!"[7]

Since 1988, an international team led by the Tubingen Professor Manfred Korfmann has been responsible for the excavations at Troy. No summer passes without some new sensation. The 90 experts or so from different faculties and countries soon ascertained that the hill of Hissarlik was inhabited without a break from the beginning of the 3rd millennium BC up to Roman times. Even the lowest layer of all, called Troy I, had an 8-foot (2.5m) thick defensive wall with three gateways. The next layers—Troy II and III—contained the remains of living quarters and terraces, as well as bronze and gold artifacts. In layers IV and V, dated 2100 to 1800 BC, the Trojans don't seem to have had a very rosy time—at least if the remains of their meals are anything to go by. There were also signs of several fires.

Troy VI was the biggest, and its date of 1800 to 1250 BC ought to make it the Troy of which Homer wrote. The excavators believe, however, that the city was destroyed by an earthquake. On the other hand, Troy VI did have several palaces, and a defensive wall that was longer and thicker than that of its precursors. But there were no signs of a fierce war such as Homer describes. There ought to be any amount of arrow and spear heads in Troy IV if this is where the famous war took place. One would also have expected to find engraved tablets, for by then writing was established.

Not until we reach Troy VII, dated at between 1200 and 1000 BC, do we find an insignificant little bronze tablet, 1 inch (2.5cm) long, engraved with some hardly decipherable "Luvic" hieroglyphs—a language related to Hittite. It seems to have been the seal of some trader. This makes it more and more likely that "Troy was in fact the same as Vilusa,"[8] as Birgit Brandau writes in her excellent book on the current state of excavations.

*Image 36: This wooden Trojan Horse
was made for tourists.*

*Image 37: The alleged site of ancient Troy. However, this was built on a very
small scale; what is lacking is monumental, massive construction.*

Image 38: The alleged site of ancient Troy.

Image 39: This theater, too, which dates back to the 4th century BC, *is not much more than a village stage.*

Image 40: In comparison with Troy's walls, here is
part of the Cyclops Wall at Delos.

But what is Vilusa? It was a place in the Hittite kingdom also men-tioned in Hittite traditions. So not Troy then? Or was Vilusa the Hittite name for Troy?

The layer of Troy VIII contained only insignificant remains from Greek times (roughly 950–85 BC), although this was the period in which the rest of Greece—the Acropolis, Delphi, and so on—flowered most ex-tensively. Then finally there was Troy IX, which arose about AD 500. This place turned out to be the same as the Roman sacred place of Ilium.

Did Homer exaggerate shamelessly, or is Schliemann's Troy not the same as that of the poet? But there was more than just the Hissarlik hill to be considered: there was also the region surrounding it. Eberhard Zangger is a geo-archaeologist—someone, therefore, who pursues archaeology from a geologist's perspective. He turned his attention from the Hissarlik hill to the landscape along the coast, and started thinking. Then he read Plato's story of Atlantis several times. Finally Zangger began counting, comparing, and bringing things together in his mind. The result was a book to which countless experts have responded with astonishing interest.[9] Eberhard aims to prove in it that Troy was really Atlantis. A bit rich, one would have thought, to assume he had solved the riddle of Atlantis. If Troy and Atlantis were the same place, why does Homer always write about Troy and the Trojan War, never once using the word Atlantis? The American archaeologist Curtiss Runnels said of Zangger's book that "it will have the same effect on the academic world as Schliemann's discoveries 100 years ago."[10] And the British archaeologist Professor Anthony Snodgrass is convinced that Zangger's comparison of Atlantis and Troy is sufficiently well founded to deserve the attention of many different specialist fields.

If Zangger is right, Atlantis-cum-Troy would not have been destroyed 9,000 years before Plato, but only about 1184 BC. Atlantis would also not have gone under in a single cataclysmic night, but would have been destroyed by the Trojan War. This is contrary to the evidence of Troy VI and Troy VII, which were not finished off by war or flooding but by an earthquake. Also Troy is on the hill of Hissarlik, and could not therefore have been submerged. So how can Eberhard Zangger equate Plato's Atlantis with Homer's Troy?

Zangger has his reasons. Whether they are really convincing is open to question.

The name "Atlantis" is well known, and for some represents a fascination, a dream, a paradise that never existed. Atlantis is like the miraculous world of childhood, a magic island of peace, a fairy-tale of a time when the world was happy and full of carefree people.

Is there more to it than just longing? Were Atlantis and Troy, as Zangger tries to demonstrate, really one and the same? What supports his ideas, what undermines them? If Zangger is wrong, does this mean that Atlantis is finally dead and buried? People have been theorizing for centuries about where it might be—and always in vain. Who started this Atlantis myth in the first place? What form did it take? Where does the original story come from?

Chapter 5
Atlantis: The Millennia-Old Whodunnit

Some people speak from experience, others speak not from experience.

—Christopher Morley, 1890–1957

It may have been in 401 BC. Athens was celebrating a festival in honor of its patron goddess. Jugglers and dancers whirled through the streets, and at the foot of the Acropolis, young actors entertained the crowds with a play. Above, in the temple of Athene, the holy flame burned. The air was heavy with incense, and fattened sacrificial beasts thronged the narrow streets. At the northern edge of the city, where the small shrine of the local hero Academos stood, five men met together in the cool inner courtyard of a spacious stone house. They knew each other well, and had already spent many nights in philosophical debate. The host, probably Plato himself, invited the guests to sit down on soft cushions. Youths served cool drinks.

Did his generation take Plato seriously? Or was he regarded as an outsider? Who were the guests? Important and honorable men, whose word counted for something, or just loud-mouths? Here is a quick guide to the participants:

- Plato: Son of Ariston, from a well-to-do Athenian family. In his younger years he wrote tragedies, until he found his way to philosophy through Socrates. For eight whole years, he attended Socrates' talks. After the latter's death, Plato visited Euclid in Megara, and studied geometry and mathematics with him. After a short residence in his home town of Athens, he traveled to Crete, Egypt, and Sicily, and was introduced at the court of Dyonysius of Syracuse. Dyonysius, a tyrant, probably didn't have much time for philosophy, for he had Plato arrested after some disagreement, and handed him over to the Spartan ambassador, who sold him as a slave. After various adventures, someone bought Plato his freedom, and he returned to Athens, the town of his birth, where he founded the Academy. Plato spent the last years of his life in high academic circles, and some of his pupils became famous. He is said to have died during a marriage feast.

- Socrates: Son of the sculptor Sophroniscos from Athens. He is regarded as the founder of Greek philosophy. His pupils came from the noblest Athenian circles. He was condemned to die by drinking a "poisoned chalice," because of supposed godlessness. He would have been able to flee, but refused to do so, because he believed the decision of the state must overrule that of the individual.

- Timaeus: Astronomer and researcher into natural phenomena from Locroi in southern Italy. According to Socrates he "showed his worth in the highest office and positions of honor in the city." Timaeus advocated the teachings and mathematics of Pythagoras.

- Critias: An older man, a highly respected politician in Athens, and one of Athens' "30 heads." Critias claims several times to have heard the Atlantis story from his grandfather—also called Critias—and to have in his possession written documents about it. Critias is related to Plato on his mother's side.

- Hermocrates: A well-known commander from Syracuse. In the Peloponnesian War, he fought on the side of Sparta. Later he was banished. (Plato experts are not in agreement about whether he is this Hermocrates or another one.)

So the drinks have been served, the participants and probably a few listeners have taken their places. Socrates opens the discussion in jovial vein:

Socrates: One, two, three—but the fourth, my dear Timaeus, of those who were yesterday the guests and today are the hosts, where has he got to?

Timaeus: He is unwell, Socrates, for if it were up to him he would never have stayed away from our gathering.

Socrates: Then it is no doubt up to you and your friends to fill his place?

Timaeus: Certainly. We others will do all we can; for it would indeed be a poor showing if we didn't gladly return your hospitality of yesterday in a fitting and worthy manner.

Socrates: So do you still remember all that I suggested you should speak about?

Timaeus: We remember a good deal of it, and if we do not, you are anyway here to remind us. The best thing, though, if you do not mind too much, would be for you to give us a short overview once more, so that we take it in properly.[1]

Then the men chat about rules which ought to be adhered to in a country. Hermocrates recalls that only the day before, Critias had told of a legend, but Socrates had no longer been present. He asks Critias to repeat it, so that they can examine it more closely. Critias then begins a long monologue, the introduction to the story of Atlantis. It is important to follow this rather long-winded account, for it reveals some of the background to the origin of the Atlantis legend. I shall use a translation by Professor Otto Apelt from the year 1922.

Critias: Socrates, this is a very strange tale you will hear, which lays claim to complete truth. Solon, the greatest of the seven wise men, assured us of this in his own day. He was actually related to my great-grandfather Dropides, and a very good friend of his, as he testifies at many places in his poems. He once told my grandfather Critias—who, when very old, passed it on to me—that there were many great and wondrous achievements of our Athenian state in past ages which the passage of time and the passing of generations had allowed to be forgotten. But the greatest of all these is one which it may now be the right moment for us to tell you, not only as thanks, but also at the same time to honor the goddess on this, her feast-day, in worthy and honest manner, as though in the form of a song of praise.

Socrates: Well spoken. But what sort of achievement was this, which Critias heard from Solon as one actually performed by our Athenian state, for it is not mentioned elsewhere in history?

Critias: I will tell you this old story, then, which I heard from a very ancient man. This was [my grandfather] Critias, who was already nearly 90, while I was at the most ten years old. He told it to me on the "Day of Youths," the Apaturien festival. For the youths, this festival took the same course as always. The Fathers assigned prizes for the reciting of poetry. A wealth of poems were recited, by all sorts of different poets. Solon's poems were new at that time, which is why many of us boys chose his songs to sing. Now one of the elders expressed the opinion to Critias—I'm not sure whether he really meant it, or if he was simply paying him a compliment—that Solon was not only the wisest, but also the most refined of all the poets. The old man—and I remember this as if it was yesterday—was very pleased indeed to hear this, and smiling replied: "Yes, Amynandros, and if he had not just pursued poetry simply in odd moments, but had applied effort and serious-ness to it like all other poets, and if he had been able to complete what he brought with him from Egypt, instead of being forced to give it up because of all the turmoil and disarray he found here on his return, I believe that he would have surpassed Hesiod, Homer, and any other poet you care to mention." "But what kind of story was this which he brought back?" asked the other. "A description," replied my grandfather, "of a mighty achievement, which deserves to outstrip the fame of everything else—one which Athens per-formed, but which has been forgotten through the passage of time and the downfall of those who achieved it, whose descendants did not survive to our own day." "Tell from the beginning," the other replied, "what Solon told you, and how and from whom he heard it as a true story."[2]

~~~

"In Egypt," began Critias, "in the delta at whose end the Nile River divides, there is a region called the Saitic, whose largest city is Sais, the birth city of King Amasis. The founder of the city is said by the inhabitants to have been a god, whose Egyptian name is Neith, but which they say is Athene in Greek. They claim that they are very well disposed to Athenians, and even to some extent related to them. This is where Solon journeyed, as he told me, and was received with all honor. When he inquired of the most knowledgeable of the priests about the origin and history of the land, it was fairly apparent that, like other Hellenes, he knew next to nothing about these things. In order to encourage them to impart information about the ancient days, he began to speak about the oldest times of Greece, the stories of Phoroneus, supposedly the most ancient man, and Niobe, and how after the Great Flood Deucalion and Pyrrha remained; then he listed their descendants and tried to give a most precise account of the number of years, relating this to the history he spoke of. Then one of the priests, a very old man, exclaimed: 'O Solon, Solon, you Hellenes are still children, and there is no such thing as an ancient Greek!' When Solon heard this, he asked, 'What do you mean by that?'

'As far as your souls are concerned, you are all young; for you do not bear with you any primeval thoughts based upon teachings which awaken reverence, nor any knowledge whose hair is grey with age. The reason for this is the following. Numerous and of many kinds are the destructions and catastrophes which have broken over the race of men, and which are still to come: the most violent through fire and water, and other lesser catastrophes through a thousand other causes. For what is told in your land, namely that Phaethon, the son of Helios, took the reins of his father's team, but was unable to follow his father's course, thus ravaging broad stretches of land with fire, and himself dying by a bolt of lightning, sounds like a folk tale, but is in fact to do with a deviation from its accustomed course of the heavenly body which encircles the earth, and with devastation of the face of the earth over long periods through massive fires. The consequence of this is that all inhabitants of mountains and high places, and all inhabitants of dry regions will be more affected by this annihilation than those who dwell beside rivers and seas. But for us the Nile, which is our savior in every way, once more protects us from such a fate, fending it off from us. When, on the other hand, the gods flood the earth with water so as to cleanse it, the inhabitants of mountainous places, the shepherds and cowherds, are spared, while the city dwellers in your lands are swept into the sea by torrents. In our country, in contrast, neither in this case nor in other ways does any water pour down from the heavens on to the fields, but everything rises up naturally from below. Therefore, and for these reasons, everything remains as it was, and so we retain memory of the most ancient days. In truth though, things are thus: in all regions where extreme cold or heat does not make it impossible, there is always a population of people, sometimes larger, sometimes smaller. Wherever it is then—whether in your country or here, or elsewhere—wherever anything magnificent or great or anything of particular interest of any kind has happened, it is recorded here in the temples in written documents, preserved against destruction from time immemorial. It is different for you and other peoples. Hardly have you developed writing and all else that civilization requires, than the heavens open their gates over you once more and pour down in torrents like a malady, only letting those escape with their lives who understand nothing of writing and have no culture or education. This is why you always become, as it were, young again, without any knowledge of what took place in ancient times, whether in your lands or ours. The course of the generations, for example as it appears in your description, Solon, is hardly different from a child's tale. For firstly you remember only a single flooding of the earth, although there have been so many before that; secondly you do not know that the best and noblest race of men dwelt in your own land. From a small vestige of this race you yourself descend, and your whole country descends. But you are unaware of this because the survivors and their descendants passed through many generations without recording anything in writing. For there were times, my Solon, before the greatest, most destructive flood, when the community now known as Athens was the best and most splendid of all, not only in regard to warfare, but also to the way it was regulated by laws, which was unsurpassed in the world. To this state of yours was ascribed the greatest deeds and best political statutes which we have ever heard of.'

When Solon heard this, he showed his astonishment, and asked the priest to tell him everything to do with these former citizens of Athens, from start to finish. But the priest replied, 'I will keep nothing from you Solon, I will tell you everything, as a favor to you and your city, but above all out of regard for the goddess who had a share both in your country and ours, and who advanced both of them, and brought them high culture: first yours, 1,000 years earlier, from the seed which she had received for this purpose from Mother Earth and Hephaistos, and then later ours. The founding of our state took place 8,000 years ago, according to the records of our temple documents. The people whose laws and most outstanding deeds I will briefly tell you of, were therefore citizens who lived 9,000 years ago. Afterwards we can take our time to consider all further specific details by perusing the documents themselves.'"[3]

In the monologue so far, Critias has mentioned the name Solon several times. Who was this man? Solon was an ancestor of Plato who was very highly regarded (often referred to as a priest). He gave the Athenians a new constitution, and in 571 BC traveled to Egypt, to Naucratis, a harbor on the Canopic stretch of the Nile. Only 10 miles (16km) away lay the temple city of Sais, where there was a translators' school. Solon said that he heard the Atlantis story from an old temple scribe called Sonchis, and at the same time saw it written in hieroglyphics. About 650 years after Solon's death, Plutarch wrote a book about him: The Life of Solon. In it Plutarch says that

Solon himself had wanted to record the Atlantis story in writing, but had been prevented from doing so by his advanced age.

In his introduction, Critias mentions a conversation which Solon had in Sais. It would seem very strange to accuse Critias of tall-storytelling; he is speaking of an experience his ancestor had, and Critias himself is one of the "30 heads of Athens," highly respected politicians. Why should he want to tell fibs to this circle of men? They were all old and wise enough to see through lies. Around the men sat pupils, and everything he said was being written down. We're not talking about the rambling introduction to a hypothesis, nor talk about an ideal republic, as is often assumed. Plato after all had described such a state in his books *Laws*, *The Republic* and *Politics*. He had already said everything, so why should he need an additional pack of lies about some Atlantis?

In addition, Critias seems to know exactly what he is talking about. He lists geographical details, such as the place where the River Nile divides, the great city of Sais, the birth town of King Amasis, and so on. And he confirms that documents and texts about Atlantis were to be found in Sais. Solon, we will later learn, also wrote down the Atlantis text from an inscription on a statue or pillar. Stories on pillars must have been particularly important ones, otherwise people would never have considered it worthwhile to immortalize them there.

Then Critias conveys to the others the words of the old priest, as he knows them from Solon. This priest assures him that the Egyptians had recorded it all in writing. In one of these texts it was reported that once, before the great flood, Athens had waged war on a power which had its base in the "Atlantic sea," for in those days this sea is said to have been navigable but was now—in Solon's time—no longer so. Why not?

Because then "behind the pillars of Heracles" there was an island, from which one could cross to the further islands behind it, and also to the "mainland on the other side." Then had come a time of "mighty earthquakes and floods," and "a day and night full of appalling terrors." The island of Atlantis had vanished, and the sea there was therefore no longer navigable, because of the "enormous masses of mud which gathered about the sinking island." Critias closes this first Atlantis story with the words: "So, my Socrates, you have now heard a very brief version of the story my grandfather Critias told me, which he had from Solon."

Almost apologetically, Critias adds that he spent the night before recalling everything, for, he says, what one learns as a youth stays in the memory. Then the men discuss matters of astronomy, geometry, and the creation of the world. Nowadays our astrophysicists talk about the "creation of time," and in Plato's *Timaeus* dialogue a similar view is expressed: "Time arose together with the universe, so that both, created simultaneously, would also be undone at the same time..."

Our own science isn't one whit sharper.

Is that all that antiquity tells us about Atlantis? No, that's only the beginning! The following day the same circle of men meets once more. In the meantime, Critias seems to have gotten his papers in order. Timaeus opens the conversation and urges Critias to continue the story of Atlantis. Critias does this, but first asks his conversation partners for understanding of the difficulties involved in recalling an old story from memory. He compares his undertaking with that of a painter, who conjures a wonderful picture onto the canvas. The picture, he says, ought to be a faithful reproduction of the original, and the same applies to oral description. He hopes to do justice to this difficult task.

I only mention this introduction to show how seriously these men viewed the Atlantis story. Each one there was aware that Critias had to relate from memory (and with the help of a few notes) a story he had learned by heart when a boy. Critias for his part was striving to recreate the picture in a way faithful to his memory of it:

Critias: Above all let us first recall that 9,000 years had passed since the war, which I will describe, was said to have broken out between those who lived beyond the pillars of Heracles and those dwelling within them. It has already been mentioned that our city of Athens was the greatest among the latter, and pursued the war to its end, while the former, the people of the island of Atlantis, were ruled by its kings. This island was, as we saw, once larger than

Libya and Asia, but now had sunk into the sea as a consequence
of earthquakes, and presented to those who wanted to sail to the
further sea an insuperable obstacle in the form of a mass of mud....[4]

This conversation took place about 400 BC. Working back from today,
the event of which Critias speaks must have occurred about 11,500 years
ago. I have already written of the "impossible dates" which the traditions
and legends of ancient peoples confront us with. At present, there is nothing
else to be done but let them stand as they are. The equation that Troy equals
Atlantis receives its first major setback at this point. According to Homer's
Iliad and Odyssey, the siege of Troy lasted 10 years. Archaeological findings speak of a devastation which occurred about 1200 BC. So in this case
only one of two things is possible:

1. Homer's and Schliemann's Troy was once called Atlantis,
    and was destroyed around 1200 BC. In this case there would
    only be a couple of hundred years between the destruction of
    Troy (or Atlantis) and Homer's account of it. So why would he
    not mention the name of Atlantis? (The same applies to other
    Greek historians.) The former names of Troy are known, right
    back to mythical times, yet the word Atlantis does not appear
    anywhere.

2. Homer's and Schliemann's Troy once had the name of Atlantis
    in a past that is lost in the mists of time. That Atlantis was
    not however identical with the "Troy" of archaeology, because
    it would have been much more ancient than Troy at the time
    of its destruction. Such an assumption would render the ar-
    chaeological finds from Schliemann's Troy useless as part of
    an "Atlantis model." Added to this, the myth is a folk-memory.
    Such a mighty city as Atlantis does not vanish from folk-mem-
    ory and suddenly change its name to Troy, Tros, or Ilion.

And what about the 9,000 years which Critias speaks of? Eberhard
Zangger thinks the Egyptians had been using a national sun calendar and
two religiously-inspired moon calendars since 2500 BC. It is likely that
the dates on the temple pillars in Sais, from which Solon wrote down his

Atlantis story, should be reckoned in moon cycles. A calculation based on this would produce a date of 1207 BC, and at that time the Greeks were indeed entangled in great wars, as part of which Troy was destroyed. This would mean that Troy/Atlantis would have had to exist up to 1207 BC. Why then does Critias (quoting Solon) emphasize that Atlantis was situated in the Atlantic Ocean? And I don't just mean the reference to the "Pillars of Heracles." Troy neither lies in the Atlantic Ocean, nor is it an island. And if I place the destruction of Troy/Atlantis in 1207 BC, the same problems arise as under point 1. It gets worse: if Atlantis/Troy existed around 1200 BC and previously held sway over a great realm, why do the Egyptians and Babylonians, who would have been close neighbors of this mighty power, know nothing about it?

In Plato's dialogue, the men continue to give ear to Critias. He mentions, as an aside—and it might almost have been something I wrote— that the gods had once divided the earth amongst themselves, into various regions. Each god had owned a particular realm, and regarded us human beings as their property, whom they could nurture and educate. Then Critias speaks about Greece before the Flood, that is, before the destruction of Atlantis. But he does not think of mentioning that Atlantis was part of the geographical region of Greece, and that it was more or less just next door. Troy is only 186 miles (300 km) from Athens, on a sea route which was much travelled in 1200 BC. It is also north-east of Athens. The Atlantic Ocean, of course, is in the opposite direction.

The wise Solon, who wrote down the Atlantis story in Sais, lived between 640 and 560 BC. The destruction of Atlantis/Troy would have taken place a mere 600 years before his time. In Egypt, Solon learned that the sea in the region of the former Atlantis was now unnavigable because of the great masses of mud there which had formed when Atlantis sank. Now the sea around Troy, together with the passage through the Dardanelles, certainly is navigable. It is actually because of its position by the sea that Troy/Atlantis is said to have blossomed and flourished. The Dardanelles were still navigable after the destruction of Troy. And if one assumes that after the destruction of Troy/Atlantis the Greeks somehow dredged the unnavigable area and made it navigable again, then the Greeks would surely know about this—for it only happened 600 short years before Solon!

Critias (or Solon) says nothing about any of that. On the contrary, he makes it quite clear that those with "Hellenic" (that is Greek) names are also from a "foreign race." And then he gives such an incredible wealth of precise details that it is only with great difficulty that one could view them as the products of fantasy:

> **Critias:** Yet I must first preface my account with a short observation, so that you are not surprised when you hear Greek names in a story concerning men of a foreign race. You will hear the reason for this. Solon, who had the intention of using these names in his poems, searched for their original meanings and found that the Egyptians—I mean those most ancient ones who had first written down these records—had translated them into their own language. Solon then pondered about each name and wrote them down, translating them once more into our language. And this written account was in the possession of my grandfather, and is now in mine, and I studied it carefully in the days of my youth. So when you hear names which are the same as ones in use in our country, you should not be surprised, for now you know the reason. The beginning of this long account goes as follows....[5]

There follows a confirmation of the truth of the written version of the Atlantis legend, to which Critias adds once more that it belonged to his grandfather and now to him.

> **Critias:** As already mentioned, when the whole earth was divided amongst the gods, some received a larger and others a smaller portion, in which to set up shrines and places of sacrifice to themselves. Poseidon received the island of Atlantis, where he gave abode to those who were descended from his union with a mortal woman, and at a place which was of the following nature. From the sea to the middle of the whole island stretched a plain, which could not have been surpassed for beauty and fertility of its soil. Besides this plain, again towards the middle of the island, about

50 stadia distant from the sea, was a mountain low on all sides. It was inhabited by one of the original earthborn men, by the name of Evenor, with his wife Leucippe. The fruit of their union was an only daughter, Cleito. When the girl reached the age of maturity, her father and mother died. But Poseidon, who had fallen in love with her, united with her, and smoothing the sides of the hill on which she lived, surrounded it with strong defenses. He placed in alternation larger and smaller rings, of earth and sea water, around each other: two of earth and three of sea water, starting from the middle of the island as though drawn with a compass, always with the same distance from each other, so that the hill became inaccessible to human beings—for there were as yet no ships or sailors. It was however perfectly easy for him, a god, to furnish the island with all that was necessary; making two springs, one warm, the other cold, pour from the earth, and nurturing manifold and abundant fruits from the soil. They had five sets of twin sons, and raised them, dividing the whole Atlantic island into ten parts. To the firstborn of the eldest pair, he gave his mother's dwelling place, with its surrounding region, the largest and best, and made him a king over the others. Yet he also made the others into rulers, giving each one dominion over many people and much land. He also gave them names. To the oldest one, the king, he gave the name from which the whole island and also the Atlantic sea takes its name: Atlas. To the second-born of the eldest pair of twins, who received the outermost part of the island, from the pillars of Heracles to the land of Gades, as it is still known in that region, he gave the name which in Greek is Eumelus, and in the native language of the country named after him, Gadeiros. Of the second pair of twins he called one Ampheres, the other Evaimon; of the third pair he named the older Mneseus, and the younger Autocthon. The elder of the fourth pair was called Elasippos, the younger Estor; the elder of the fifth pair, finally, he called Azaes, and the younger Diaprepes. These and their descendants lived there for many generations, not only as rulers over many other islands in the ocean, but also, as already mentioned, as masters over those living within the pillars

of Heracles, as far as Egypt and Tyrrhenia. Atlas, then, brought
forth a numerous and highly favored race. The kingship always
passed down from eldest to eldest, and was perpetuated through
many generations. At the same time, they amassed great wealth
and riches, such as were probably never seen before, nor will be
again in future times, and provided everything which the city or
the rest of the land might need. Much was brought to them from
other lands subject to their dominion, but the island supplied most
of their needs. Firstly, everything which is produced by mining the
earth, in the way of minerals and workable metals, including a type
of metal which we now only know by name, but which was then
more than a mere name, orichalcum or gold-copper ore. This was
obtained from the earth at many places, and next to gold was most
prized by this ancient race.[6]

Even though Critias makes it clear that the names in this story have
been translated into Greek, there is not a single one here that is familiar to
us from the Troy legend. Next Critias explains that in this land of Atlantis
all trees and fruits, as well as all vegetables, grew wonderfully well. Why?
"Because its climate in those days united the sun's warmth with moisture."
That does not fit with the climate of Troy, where it is unpleasantly cold
in winter; tropical fruits and trees would not survive there. They did in
Atlantis, though, the whole year through. Finally Critias begins to talk
about the architecture and buildings of Atlantis.

And his account is so precise that architects of our own day have been
able to make accurate, scale drawings from them.[7]

Critias: Firstly they made bridges over the rings of water which
surrounded the original ancient city, in order to make a path to and
from the king's palace. And the king's palace itself they built at
the dwelling place of the god and their ancestors. Each succeeding
king received it from his predecessor, and added to and adorned it
more richly than it had been before—until, through the greatness
and beauty of their works, they had made their dwelling a marvel
to behold. Then, beginning from the sea, they dug a canal 3 plethra
wide, 100 feet deep, and 50 stadia long, as far as the outermost

ring, so that ships could sail in as into a harbor, and they made the entrance large enough for the largest vessels to enter. Thus they broke through the rings of earth too, which separated the rings of water from each other, so that one could sail from one to another in a trireme. But they constructed bridges over these openings, so that the vessels passed under the bridges, for the banks of the earth-rings were raised high enough above the water to allow this. The largest of the rings, into which the sea flowed, had a breadth of 3 stadia, and the next earth-ring had the same dimensions. The water-ring of the second pair was 2 stadia wide, as was the dry ring also. The water-ring closest to the middle of the island was 1 stadium wide. But the island on which the king's palace stood was 5 stadia in diameter. They surrounded this with a stone wall, and the earth-rings likewise, from one side of a 1-plethron-wide bridge to the other, placing towers and bridges on the passages to the sea. The stones they used, some white, some black, and some red, they quarried from the under edges of the island in the middle, and from both the inside and outside edges of the rings. At the same time as quarrying, they also hollowed out shelters and docks for ships, on both sides of the rings, which were roofed by the overhanging rocks that remained. Some of the buildings which they constructed were of a single color; others were built of varicolored stones, to please the eye, in compositions which had a natural charm. Then they overlaid the entire outermost wall with bronze, spreading it in a similar way to anointing oil. The next wall they coated with tin and the innermost wall which surrounded the palace they plated with gold-copper ore, or orichalcum, which had a burnished and fiery sheen.[8]

Things get more complicated. What are we meant to make of "3 plethra" or "1 stadium"?

Greek measurements of length
1 foot = 30 centimeters
100 feet = 1 plethron (30 m)
3 plethra = 98 yards (90 m)
6 plethra = 197 yards (180 m or 1 stadium)
1 stadium = 197 yards (180m)
5 stadia = 985 yards (900 m)
50 stadia = 5.5 miles (9 km)
2,000 stadia = 223 miles (360 km)
10,000 stadia = 1,116 miles (1,800 km)
Greek measurements of area
1 los = 2,153 sq. yards (1,800 sq. m)
1 kleros = about 815 acres (3.24 sq km or roughly 330 hectares)

Assuming Critias is not just repeating some fantasy of his grandfather, Atlantis must be of amazing proportions. We need to remember several salient points:

- The gods divide the world between them. Poseidon gets Atlantis.

- About 50 stadia (5.5 miles or 9 km) from the shore there rises a low mountain which is accessible from all sides.

- Its first inhabitants are the earth-born Evenor and Leucippe. Their only daughter, Cleito, loses her parents.

- Poseidon gets Cleito pregnant.

- Poseidon surrounds the "low" mountain with strong defenses composed of alternating rings of water and earth, which are "inaccessible to human beings."

- Poseidon and Cleito have five pairs of male twins. The oldest son is called Atlas. It is from him that the Atlantic Ocean gets its name.

- The island is rich in metals.

- The climate is subtropical ("sun-warmth and moisture").

- Atlas and his descendants build a king's palace or castle in the center of the island.

- From the sea is built a canal 50 stadia (5.5 miles/9 km) long, and 3 plethra (98 yards/90 m) wide, as far as the first ring.

- The largest ring is 3 stadia broad (590 yards/5401m).

- The diameter of the centre of the island is 5 stadia (985 yards/900m).

- This center is surrounded by a stone wall, which is covered in metal.

- Towers, gateways, and houses are built in different colors: (white, black, red).

- Docks are built to shelter ships, with overhanging cliff roofs.

- The wall around the central palace is coated in "gold-copper ore."

There are already a few problems in reconciling Atlantis with Troy, but it is still not impossible. Everything ultimately depends on whether Critias is telling a pretty tale from his grandfather's time, or a true story, and I will come back to this. If Atlantis and Troy were the same, there would have to be a defensive wall around Troy I composed of "rings of water and earth," which were "inaccessible to human beings." The archaeological excavations did indeed expose a defensive wall around Troy I, but not one worthy of the god Poseidon. No ring of water was found close to the center, and such a ring would not suit the type of hill it is anyway.

Once again, Atlantis ought to lie in the Atlantic Ocean, to which it gave the name. As we know, Troy is in a quite different location. The climate of Troy is not subtropical, and so far no 5.5-mile (9km) long canal has been found leading to the center of the inner ring. However, extensive excavations and measurement have not yet been undertaken on Troy's environs.

The center of Atlantis is meant to have been 985 yards (900m) in diameter—that part could fit with Troy, though not the bit about the walls being covered entirely in metal (ore). It is possible, though, that over years metals might have been stolen or melted down, or could have been destroyed by fire. Traces would be present in the soil, which could be tested by taking samples. Schliemann claims that at a depth of about 30 feet (9m) he came across a slag layer of melted lead and copper ore, but this was never confirmed by current excavations.

Finally, there should be buildings in three different colors—which have so far not been found - and the central palace ought to be coated with a gold-copper alloy—orichalcum. There was no sign of this. All that is certain is that Homer does not mention any such thing in his epic. But Critias has not yet finished his tale:

Critias: The royal dwelling place within the citadel was arranged as follows. In the middle there was a temple dedicated to Cleito and Poseidon, closed to public view, which was surrounded with a golden wall. This was where the race of 10 princes had once been begotten and born. There, each year, from all 10 zones of the island, were brought the firstborn as offerings to each of the 10 families of descendants. The temple of Poseidon was 1 stadium long, 3 plethra broad, and a height pleasing to the eye, yet its whole form could not conceal a certain affinity with barbarism. They covered the whole exterior of the temple with silver, apart from the pinnacles which were of gold. As far as the interior is concerned, the ivory ceiling was adorned all over with gold, silver and orichalcum, and the rest—walls, pillars, and floor—was coated in orichalcum too. They also raised golden statues, of the god himself on a chariot, driving a team of six winged horses, and of such a size that his head touched the ceiling; and around about him 100 Nereids on dolphins, for that is the number which the people of that time believed there to be. There were also numerous statues which had been given as offerings by private individuals. Around the temple stood many other golden images—of the women and all others who were descended from the 10 kings, and many other great offerings, both from kings and private individuals, some from the town itself, some from those living beyond its borders, who were under its dominion. The altar also corresponded in size and kind to the rest of this magnificence, and the king's quarters likewise reflected the grandeur of the kingdom. The springs, one of hot and one of cold water, provided an inexhaustible supply, and each in its own manner was of very fine taste and goodness. These waters were used in the most efficient way. In their close proximity buildings were raised, and suitable trees planted. They also constructed water containers or cisterns, some in the open air, others in enclosed rooms for taking warm baths in the winter. The bathing rooms for the king and his subjects were separate from one another, as were the rooms for women and those for horses, and those for cattle, each type of room adorned in the way which suited its purpose. The water which ran off was channeled into the grove of Poseidon, whose soil was full of goodness, and whose trees of the most varied kind grew wonderfully high. All remaining water was diverted through aqueducts over the bridges to the outer earth-rings. In the area of these water channels were numerous shrines for many gods, as well as gardens and wrestling courts, both for the gymnastic exercises of the men themselves and for exercises with teams of horses, separate ones on each of the two earth rings. In the middle of the larger island there was also an excellent racecourse, 1 stadium broad, and its length extending around the whole island to allow full scope for horse-teams to race. Around this, on both sides, were the living quarters for the majority of subjects. The most trustworthy were given guard duties on the smaller earth-ring, closer to the citadel. And those who were loyal above all others had their dwellings in the citadel itself, in the immediate proximity of the king. The docks were full of triremes and all that is necessary for equipping them. Now leaving the king's palace and citadel behind, and passing the three outer harbors, one came to a wall which began at the sea and encircled everything, being everywhere 50 stadia distant from the largest ring and harbor, and meeting itself again where it began, at the mouth of the canal which led to the sea. This whole area was full of dwellings, and the largest harbor was chockablock with ships and traders, who arrived there from many different places, and whose shouts, din and clatter kept going day and night. I have described the town and the ancient citadel more or less as it was told to me, and now I must turn to the rest of the country and its character, and the way it was governed. The whole region was described to me as high and with steep cliffs sloping to the sea, with only the area around the town being a level plain. This plain surrounding the city was surrounded by mountains, which descended to the sea. It formed a smooth and even area, of a longish, rectangular shape, 3,000 stadia in length and 2,000 stadia in breadth across the middle. This part of the island faced south, protected from the north winds. But the mountains which surrounded it, if we are to believe the inhabitants' hymns of praise, were greater in number, size, and beauty than any that we know now. These mountainous regions contained many places where people lived in large numbers, as well as rivers, lakes, and meadows offering nourishment to tame and wild animals of all kinds, and wooded areas whose rich variety of trees provided an inexhaustible supply of raw materials for all craftsmen. The natural formation of the plain, which many kings had improved over long periods, was as follows. Its shape was that of a regular, longish rectangle, and what was lacking in nature had been supplied by the hand of man in the form of a ditch dug all around it. The depth, width, and length of this sound incredible and impossible for the work of human beings to accomplish, but I must tell you what I heard, namely that it was 1 plethron deep, and everywhere 1 stadium wide. The length of the ditch, running all around the plain, was 10,000 stadia. It collected the waters streaming down from the mountains, which, encircling the plain and touching the town on two sides, ran into the sea in the following way. Straight canals were dug, most of them 100 foot broad, which joined to the main ditch and carried the water down to the sea. Each of these channels was 100 stadia distant from the next. These were used to transport wood from the mountains to the city, and also to bring other produce of the country to the ships, through connecting channels which they laid diagonally to run between the main channels, and into the city. They had a twice-yearly harvest, which was made possible in winter by the rain which Zeus provided, and in summer by the irrigation water which they diverted from the channels.... The following arrangements were made from the very beginning for governing. Each of the 10 kings ruled in his own region, and from his own city, over the inhabitants there, and made most of the laws in that region, so that he could punish and execute whom he liked. They arranged their joint ruling in the way ordained by Poseidon, as had been passed down to them by law and through the inscriptions which the primeval fathers had engraved on a pillar cast in orichalcum. This stood in the middle of the island, in the shrine to Poseidon. It was there that the 10 gathered, alternating between every fifth and every sixth year so as not to favor an odd number above an even, and talked together and took council with one another about the affairs of each region. They also looked into whether any of them had transgressed in any way, and passed judgment if this were so. If they decided to pass judgment, though, they gave each other a solemn pledge in the following way. In the holy area of Poseidon there were bulls which roamed freely. The 10, after praying to the god that he should let them catch a sacrificial offering, took part in a hunt, but one which used no iron, only sticks and cords. The bull which they caught, though, they took to the pillar and slaughtered on the top of it, above the inscription. Upon the pillar there was, apart from the inscription, also an oath which invoked terrible curses on anyone who did not abide by the laws. After sacrificing all parts of the bull to the god, they cast into the wine in a mixing bowl prepared for this purpose one drop of blood for each of them, and consigned the rest to the fire, after washing and cleansing the pillar and the area around it. Then they dipped golden ladles into the bowl, and, pouring a libation onto the fire, swore they would judge in accordance with the laws inscribed on the pillar, and pass sentence if any of them was guilty of transgression. They also swore that they would not intentionally overstep the mark in future, would rule only lawfully, and would not obey another ruler who did not follow the laws of their father Poseidon. After each of them had sworn this for himself and his descendants, he drank and dedicated the drinking ladle to the shrine of the god. Then they ate and washed. But the moment it grew dark, and the sacrificial fire had burned low, each dressed

himself in a dark blue robe of wondrous beauty, then sitting by the
embers from the sacrifice, and extinguishing all fires around the
shrine, they received and gave judgment if any one of them was
accused of misdemeanor. The judgment they passed was inscribed
at dawn upon a golden tablet, which they raised as memorial there,
together with their robes. There were various other laws about the
rights and duties of the separate kings, but the most important were
that they must never wage war upon each other, and must always
be ready to give aid to each other if someone should try to destroy
the race of kings. They also had to take council together, as did
their forefathers, about war and other undertakings, and leave the
final decision to the descendants of Atlas. But the king should not
have the right to condemn one of his relatives to death, unless at
least six of the 10 rulers gave their consent. This mighty and magnificent power, which held sway in those regions at that time, was
later directed against our own regions in warfare, and, we have
been told, for the following reason. For many generations, as long
as divine nature still made itself felt within them, they remained
obedient to the laws and did not deny their divine origin. For their
spirits were lofty, truthful, and generous. They bore strokes of destiny with composure, and related to one another with kindness and
interest. They regarded virtue alone as being of true worth, and
therefore did not overvalue their goods and possessions, did not
prize too highly the masses of gold and other treasures, which
seemed to them more of a burden than anything else. They were
thus far from being power-crazy or out of control. They had a clear,
sober understanding that all this outer wealth could only be sus-
tained when underpinned by friendship and virtue, and would disappear if all attention and value were focused on riches alone.
Because of this attitude and the continuing influence of the divine
nature within them, everything thrived in the way I have already
described. But as the divine part of their nature increasingly vanished, diluted by frequent unions with mortals, so that a human
type of thinking prevailed, they began to be uneasy with their lot.
They grew degenerate and debased themselves in the eyes of all

who were capable of true judgment. To those, however, who had no clear power of insight into a life based on true happiness, they appeared more and more magnificent and praiseworthy, since they began to dedicate themselves to avarice and lust for power. The god of the gods, however, Zeus, who rules according to laws, and who has a sharp eye for such things, decided to rein their excesses by punishing them, for he grieved to see such a worthy race falling so low, and hoped that they might still be brought to their senses and change their ways. So he called all the gods together into their holy of holies, which is situated in the center of the whole world, and allows the gods to see into everything which is happening everywhere, and directed to those assembled there the following words.[9]

What a place to end! What words did Zeus speak to them? We'd all like to know of course, not only us but also the last 2,400 years' worth of philosophers, philologists, and Atlantis researchers. But Plato's Atlantis dialogue ends abruptly at this point; hard to understand really, for Plato wrote other things after this dialogue. Why is the end of the Atlantis story missing? Isn't there any alternative version from antiquity? Didn't any other authors tell of Atlantis?

The first reference to Atlantis which I found outside of Plato was, of all places, in the *Argonautica* by Apollonius of Rhodes:

In the evening they came ashore on the Atlantides Island. Orpheus begged them not to spurn the solemnities of the island, nor the secrets, the laws, customs, the religious rites and works. If they observed these they would be assured of the love of heaven on their further voyage over the dangerous ocean. But to speak further of these things I do not dare.[10]

Unmistakable news of an island with the name "Atlantides," where there are particular customs, and also secrets. Whereas Apollonius is usually glad of an opportunity to describe geographical and topographical features, here he falls strangely silent, not "daring" to speak more. Strange.

Perhaps we should recall the fact that Atlantis was the island of the god Poseidon, and that two of his sons were on board the Argo.

Herodotus (490–425 BC) has nothing to say about Atlantis, but in Book IV of his *Histories* (Chapters 184 and 185) he writes about a salt area that borders on a mountain region by the name of "Atlas":

> It is narrow and circular and is said to be so high that one cannot see its summits. Clouds always wreathe it, both in summer and winter. The natives say that these mountains are the pillars of heaven. The people dwelling here are called "Atlantens" after these mountains....[11]

Shortly after Plato's death, Aristotle (384–322 BC) who was one of his pupils, published a book in which he cast doubt on the truth of the Atlantis story.[12] Already then! Yet the same Aristotle also mentioned an unknown island in the Atlantic, which he called "Antilia." Another pupil of Plato was called Crantor of Soloi (330–275 BC). He is supposed to have travelled to Egypt, to Sais, and likewise seen there the written version of the Atlantis story. Grantor was the first to publish Plato's dialogues.

All later pre-Christian poets and historians of note mention Atlantis somewhere or other, including such people as Proclos, Plutarch, Poseidonius, Longinus, Strabo, Thucydides, Timagenes, Pliny, and even Diodorus Siculus. But none of them have anything to add, they all just refer to Plato. So before we go any further we have to ask whether Plato just offloaded a literary fairy tale onto the world.

The school of philosophy surrounding Plato was dedicated to truth. All his dialogues have the same aim: to get at the truth. Anyone reading Plato's works meets this search for truth at every turn. The participants analyze, compare, contradict, assume, define, and go round and round their subjects until they have been done to death. And on occasions when the conversation takes a more imaginary turn, speaking for instance of things which "might" be possible, or which one "could" imagine, then the subjunctive is used. Why would Plato diverge from this clear framework in the case of the Atlantis story? He and the other participants must have known if the story was only a fabrication, something merely invented by the Egyptians, and would surely have mentioned it. But the opposite is the case. Critias begins the dialogue by expressly stating that although the story is strange it has a "claim to be wholly true." And Socrates then asks "What sort of achievement was this, which Critias heard from Solon as one actually performed by our Athenian state, for it is not mentioned elsewhere in history?" A little later, to make absolutely sure, it is asked from whom Solon heard all this "as a true story."

The ancient Egyptian priest, who told Solon the story, emphasized that it was set down in writing in the long-distant past. And he insists that they should afterwards examine the full details with the help of the original documents. Would Plato have made up all these lies to create a more credible story?

There were also young men attending the dialogues, and perhaps other members of the public. On the second day, this worthy gentleman Critias claims to have spent the previous night recalling everything as clearly as he can. If this is a lie it is brazen. And then he insists that the written account of the Atlantis story was in his grandfather's possession, and is now in his. If these were not all Critias' own words, then Plato must have invented them. Unthinkable of someone like Plato, whose life was dedicated to the pursuit of truth.

The same Plato would then also have had to falsely attribute the Atlantis story to Solon, one of the most outstanding personalities of Athens, who was also known as a law-maker! And would Critias have stood by quietly and let Plato take the name of his grandfather in vain to back up a pack of lies? And if Critias himself had attributed a wholly false story to his grandfather, then the other participants in the dialogue would surely have contradicted him. The only other possibility is that Plato invented the whole dialogue, together with its participants. But this could hardly have been carried out, for the people mentioned in it were all alive, and every one of them had enough personality and courage to prevent their name being used in such a tissue of lies.

None of this fits with the Platonic search for truth. The same applies to the story itself. It mentions a type of metal, "orichalcum," which later no longer existed. Why invent something like that? In Atlantis there is said to have been a region "protected from the north winds." Such details are superfluous in a false story about a supposed "ideal state." Who would care which direction the wind blew from? In the center of Atlantis is said to have stood a pillar or statue, on which were engraved the laws of Poseidon. Just another perfidious lie? On this pillar there was also supposed to be inscribed an oath with dreadful curses. Why should such a thing figure in an imaginary "ideal state"? The kings of Atlantis are said a to have met to pass judgment on themselves, and to have inscribed the judgment on a golden tablet. And in the case of war, "the race of Atlas" should have the last word. What use, what moral function could it have had for the Athenians to hear about such things?

The whole story is told in the past tense, just as if it all actually happened. If it is not true this does not fit with the Platonic school's approach. Why should this school (or Plato on his own) try to sell a web of deceit to the intellectual elite of Athens? Why should he put words into the mouth of Critias, one of the most highly regarded men of his day?

I can go on—and I will for a bit longer! Critias also has the cheek to claim that the "divine" element of the descendants of Poseidon increasingly vanished because it was diluted through unions with mortals, so that eventually a "human" way of thinking got the upper hand. Who needs to know that? If it was an invention, people of those days might well have regarded it as an insult to the gods. The Atlantis story simply cannot be seen as so much poppycock invented by Plato, even if we want to assume that he used the name of living people under false pretenses.

And now along comes Eberhard Zangger and identifies Atlantis as Troy. The prerequisite for that, of course, is that Zangger take Plato seriously—in other words, believes in the Atlantis story. Umm...not altogether. Plato refers to Atlantis as an island; but Troy, of course, is not on an island. Zangger has a good explanation ready.[13] He believes that the Egyptians regarded all strangers as coming from "islands." The word "island" he suggests, had a different meaning in the Bronze Age than it does today. Because there weren't really any islands in Egypt there was no hieroglyph to represent the word; the hieroglyph used for "island" meant only a foreign, non-Egyptian coast or shore.

That may be true. But the Egyptians did know that Greece, with which they actively traded, had many small islands as well as a mainland. And the thing that really sticks in my gullet about the Atlantis/Troy equation is the power, greatness, and size of Plato's Atlantis. It is described as a thoroughly organized state, a huge region with enormous forces, far and away outstripping anything that little Troy, on the opposite coast to Egypt, could have mustered, even in its heyday.

Herodotus, for example, learns an enormous amount on his Egyptian travels. He notes down the names of the kings and dynasties, writes up periods, gods, and legends. But none of the Egyptian historians or priests inform their guest from Greece about the Atlantis that is supposed to have been just opposite them. Herodotus was hungry for knowledge; he could never learn enough, never ask enough questions. But at no point was he tempted to ask about Atlantis, because there was never an Atlantis in the geographical region of Greece, even if it later changed its name to Troy, Tros, or Ilion. The word "Atlantis" is meant to come from "Atlas," and to have given the Atlantic Ocean its name. How could it have done this if it was called Troy, Tros or Ilion? And if, as Homer tells us, a great war was waged around Troy, into which the Greeks heroically threw themselves, in which more than 1,000 ships were involved, then they would surely have known that they were destroying Atlantis and the descendants of Poseidon, and not just some barbarians.

Eberhard Zangger found various swamps, harbors, and even canals in the plain in front of Troy, and he shows in a sketch that Plato's Atlantis could easily be transposed onto it. But the same could be said of many other places. Even if excavations around Troy bring to light some ring-shaped canals, we would still have no proof that it is Plato's Atlantis. There were many cities with ring-shaped canals and defensive walls. Herodotus describes how the king of the Medeans, Deioces, had a similar site built (Book I, Chapter 98):

He built a great, strong citadel, which is today called Agbatana, in which walls stand within each other. This citadel is arranged in such a way that each succeeding ring is always higher than the previous one...the town has seven ring-walls altogether. In the innermost stands the king's palace and the treasure houses the pinnacles of the first wall are white, those of the second black, of the third purplish-red, of the fourth blue, of the fifth bright red....[14]

Is this Atlantis? Or Troy? No, it is Agbatana!

Their temple has the following appearance: it lies upon an island from the Nile two channels lead there...the forecourt of the temple is 10 fathoms high and adorned with remarkable images...around the temple runs a wall decorated with reliefs.[15]

Is this Atlantis? Troy? No. Herodotus was here describing the temple of Bubastis in Egypt. I could go on. Many temples stood on islands and were surrounded by channels. This at least tells us that the Egyptians knew what an island was!

The same Herodotus converses with Egyptian priests about the theft of Helen from Troy/Ilion (Book II, Chapters 13 onward). Even the names Homer and Iliad are expressly mentioned. But nowhere does it occur to Herodotus or the priests he is talking with to mention Atlantis and Troy in the same breath, or to say that Troy was once called Atlantis millennia ago.

So either the Atlantis story is a pure invention by Plato, which is very hard to believe, or Plato's Atlantis cannot have been called Troy. What Eberhard Zangger claimed for Troy has also been claimed by others for the islands of Crete and Santorini. The Greek seismologist Angelos Galanopoulos and his colleague Edward Bacon produced good arguments to suggest that the volcanic island of Santorini could correspond with Plato's descriptions of Atlantis,[16] and that it was simply destroyed by a volcanic eruption. Unfortunately, Plato's measurements do not fit Santorini. The authors get around this by saying that Solon got his figures wrong, and read the hundreds as thousands. As Jorg Dendl comments in an excellent Atlantis critique, however, this assumption cannot be correct:

Plato describes the division of the "great plain" very precisely. The whole country [Atlantis] was separated into portions or plots. The size of each was 10 square stadia, and there were 60,000 of these. These 60,000 plots, each one 10 × 10 stadia, can only fit into an area of 2,000 × 3,000 stadia. If Solon had read his numbers wrong, this sum would not work.[17]

And the Irish professor John Luce, who is an expert in Greek literature, placed Atlantis very plausibly on the island of Crete in Minoan times.[18, 19] The stimulus for this was the description of the bull-hunt on Atlantis "with only sticks and cords" and the sacrifice to the god Poseidon. Where was there a bull-cult in ancient times? On Crete of course! You remember, no doubt, that Zeus swam to Crete in the form of a bull with Europa on his back, and that Daedalus built a labyrinth to hold the human-headed Minotaur bull. So Atlantis must be Crete. At both places there were "mystical kings," and in both places a culture flourished which held sway over the rest of the world for long ages. In both places, too, there were splendid palaces and also of course man-made canals.

Troy/Atlantis, Santorini/Atlantis, Crete/Atlantis. Why not throw Malta in as well? But all the Mediterranean islands which are thought to be Atlantis have one disadvantage: they do not lie in the Atlantic Ocean. And Plato's dates—9,000 years old—naturally do not fit in with any of these Atlantis illusions. The Minoan palaces of Crete were destroyed around 1450 BC. Either we accept Plato as he is, or we start filtering out from his account everything which doesn't fit in with our own favorite theory.

The same Professor John Luce, the ancient Greek expert who places Atlantis in Crete, draws attention to the fact that Plato never referred to the story as "muthos" or "legend," but always as "logos" or "true word."[20] The story of the bull-hunt on Atlantis and the sacrifice of the bull on a giant pillar, incidentally, is very hard to reconcile with the idea that Plato invented it all to conjure up an "ideal state."

Most of the men whom we call "historians of antiquity" travelled through Egypt; not only Herodotus was there, but also his colleagues Diodorus, Pliny and Strabo, among others. Why did they hear nothing about Atlantis? They all gave extensive accounts of Egyptian history, and each of them was surprised by the "impossible dates" of the Egyptian dynasties. Does this not speak against Atlantis? Wouldn't at least one of these historians have brought an Atlantis story home with him?

This objection can be used both for and against Atlantis. If the Atlantis story had been common knowledge in Egypt, then others besides Solon would have heard about it. Perhaps they did hear of it, and didn't believe it. Or those 9,000 years were the reason that hardly anyone in Egypt remembered the story. That would make the old priest in Sais an exception, the one who told Solon the story and supported it with documents and an inscription. These must have been documents which were only easily available in Sais—which doesn't mean that they didn't exist elsewhere at some point. I don't really want to go over old ground again, but whole ancient libraries were destroyed—or otherwise never located. I am still hoping for the miracle that will allow one of them to turn up some day.

A few years ago, an exciting proof that Atlantis really existed was presented in a TV program (I am still waiting for the book to be published). The geologists William Ryan and Walter Pittmann say that they examined the seafloor off the northern coast of the Black Sea, and the coastline itself, by drilling and analyzing samples. Astonished, they came to the conclusion that the sea-level had risen by 492 feet (150 m), both at the coast north of the Crimean peninsula and on the coast of western Ukraine. This rise is said to have taken place in a sudden, dramatic, apocalyptic fashion, about 7,500 years ago, and was probably caused by a meteorite hitting the earth, melting millions of tons of ice and sending huge masses of water washing over the world. This apocalyptic flood had first poured through the Bosphorus and then formed the Black Sea, which had previously been an inland lake.

I cannot judge whether these two experts are right, and it is not up to me to assess whether their data are correct. What I do know is that other geologists and glacier researchers are convinced that the exact opposite is true. Professor Herbert E Wright of the University of Minnesota says: "The Atlanteans will have to search elsewhere for their catastrophes,"[21] for, he claims, it can be clearly proven that no such disaster occurred in the last

12,000 years. This is not to dispute that the sea-level really has risen—but this occurred gradually throughout the course of human history. It would be helpful if the glaciologists and oceanographers would put all their data on the table. Atlantis in the depths of the Black Sea? But the Black Sea does not lie "beyond the pillars of Heracles," as Plato claims Atlantis does, nor does it have a subtropical climate.

And while I am on the subject of ice-melting, let me mention its opposite: refrigeration. The authors Fritz Nestke and Thomas Riemer place Atlantis slap bang on the continent of Antarctica.[22] Naturally they have good reasons to support their ideas. But who doesn't? Almost anything is possible where Atlantis is concerned.

Only Eberhard's assumption that Atlantis was nothing other than Troy is hard to sustain. Whether Atlantis or Troy, both places must have been founded by someone at some time. The founder of Atlantis was called Poseidon, and he was a son of Zeus. Why did he found Atlantis? At the very beginning of the Atlantis story Poseidon is said to have fallen in love with an earthly woman Cleito, who lived on a hill, which Poseidon then surrounded with "strong defenses" which were "inaccessible to human beings" (Critias). If the founding of Atlantis was identical with the founding of Troy, then Troy I, built round 3000 BC, ought to have a strong defensive wall. But it doesn't. Certainly nothing like the Atlantis story makes out, with its rings of seawater and earth encircling one another, at equal intervals as though drawn with a compass. Such constructions would be quite impossible in the region surrounding present-day Troy. The hill of Hissarlik, on which the (supposed) Troy stands, slopes down gently to the sea on one side, and on the other side gets lost in the flat terrain, which is about 50 feet (15m) above sea-level. Poseidon's circles would have to exist on the side facing the sea, but there is nothing of the kind there. Unless, of course, the ingenious son of the gods constructed a system to pump up seawater to a higher level. If so, evidence of the rings of water ought to be clearly visible in the terrain.

Why did Poseidon construct his "strong defenses inaccessible to human beings" and his ring ditches? To found for his wife and descendants of divine blood a kingdom where they could live well and securely in the future. In that case, there ought to be traces at Troy of this mighty kingdom of Atlantis, but there aren't. Did Poseidon want to control ship traffic through the Dardanelles from the very beginning? No, for there were as yet "no ships or sailors" (Critias).

And those who see only the ruins of Troy on the hill of Hissarlik seek reasons for its founding at this spot too. Why here? Supposedly because this place had strategic importance, enabling watch to be kept on the entrance to the Dardanelles. But I'm afraid this is nonsense. Around 3000 BC, Troy I was nothing more than an insignificant little settlement, which couldn't possibly have controlled traffic into the Dardanelles. The hill of Hissarlik does not actually lie at the strategic point but some miles distant from it. In the third millennium BC, there were neither cannons nor other such weapons to prevent ships entering the Dardanelles.

There is, after all, a reason why contemporary fortifications for controlling the Dardanelles were located directly beside the entry channel, or as near as makes no difference. It would have been a joke for the town community of Troy I to try halting potential blockade-busters with small ships sent out from the hill of Hissarlik or the coast. The reason for the Troy I settlement cannot possibly have been to control the Dardanelles, for it would have to have been in a quite different place!

And Atlantis certainly doesn't fit with Troy I, as we have seen. According to the archaeological excavations, Troy is said to have been founded around 3000 BC. In the following centuries and millennia, the settlement became an increasingly fortified site. At the same time, on the other side of the Mediterranean, a phenomenal Egyptian civilization was taking shape. The Egyptians built their great pyramid 500 years after the founding of Troy. And soon the Phoenicians were dominating sea travel in the Mediterranean. If Eberhard Zangger is right about Troy and Atlantis, and this Atlantis was destroyed in the Trojan War around 1207 BC, then all Mediterranean ships must have continually sailed past it up until that time. Or, still more absurd, if Atlantis had been an island in the Mediterranean, then these seafaring peoples would continually have circumnavigated one coast or another of this mysterious Atlantis. The whole Mediterranean and its hinterland would have been involved in trading with the place. Strange, isn't it, that no one had heard of it?

Critias describes the terrain of Atlantis as generally high, and plunging down sharply to the sea. Only the area around the city was flat. "This plain surrounding the city was itself surrounded by mountains, which descended to the sea." There is no such landscape in the vicinity of Troy. The temple in the center of Atlantis was said to be 1 stadium long and 3 plethra wide, which is equal to an area of 197 × 98 yards (180m × 90m). There is no structure in the whole of Troy that is anything like this. Excavated Troy is a muddle of rooms of no particular size, certainly not of monumental dimensions, and without any wall that one could possibly call "Cyclopic" in stature. Troy's walls—from whatever layer—bear no comparison at all to the 20-foot (6 m) thick Cyclopic wall of Mycenae, or the massive domed "treasure house of Atreus." They are nothing like the phenomenal stone slabs under the temple of Apollo at Delphi, or the megalithic wall of Delos.

And the walls of Troy I are absolutely unworthy of a god such as Poseidon. The legend says that Apollo had a hand in building the wall of Troy. Just compare pictures of the megalithic wall at Delos with the humble excuse of a wall at Troy, and you will see the difference. Delos was also dedicated to Troy, and is part of the geometrical network that stretches across Greece, whereas Troy is not. Wherever these sons of the gods were active—Poseidon in Atlantis or his brother Apollo in Troy—the place which has been called Troy since the days of Heinrich Schliemann shows no sign of their activity.

As I have mentioned several times, Troy lies a few miles away from the entrance to the Dardanelles. At the Dardanelles begins the narrow seaway from the Mediterranean (the Aegean part of it) to the Sea of Marmara, on whose coast lies Istanbul. From there the Bosphorus connects to the Black Sea. This is certainly an important seaway. If Poseidon's Atlantis had been established there, then Critias or Solon would have known about it. In the Atlantis story, all other important geographical and topographical details are recorded. It is unthinkable that such an important location as this would have meant nothing for Atlantis and would therefore have been omitted from the tale. Yet Critias or Solon know nothing about it being there. Atlantis was neither founded beside a narrow seaway, nor did this once powerful realm rule over such a channel in later times.

Of course, the hinterland of Atlantis must have profited from the wealth of this legendary country. In relation to Troy this hinterland would have consisted of Ezine in the south, Cumcale in the north (right beside the channel to the Dardanelles) or Bayramic in the east. We ought to be able to find any number of relics from antiquity in an extensive circle around Troy/Atlantis. One has to remember that Troy was destroyed in 1207 BC, so the hinterland civilizations of Troy would have existed at that time. According to Homer only, Troy was destroyed in the Trojan War. So where are these splendid places which thrived on the wealth of Atlantis? There is nothing to be found in the hinterland of the "Troy" of today. And anyone who argues that Atlantis was located at the same place as Troy occupied much later on, cannot then link Homer's Trojan War with the downfall of Atlantis. The further back we go into the past, the less likely the possibility that Troy could have been Atlantis. The excavated layers of the hill of Hissarlik show this clearly.

And one thing more: if Troy was Atlantis, wouldn't the Argonauts have passed by it? In the *Argonautica* there are endless geographical details: the land of Colchis, with the mouth of the river Phasis, beside the town of Aia, where the Golden Fleece lay, is supposed to have been situated at the further end of the Black Sea. The Argonauts would therefore have had to sail right through the Dardanelles, for there is no other way to get there, and so would have come into contact with great Atlantis! But the only passage in the *Argonautica* in which any mention is made of "Atlandides" is definitely about an island and not the coast near Troy. ("In the evening they came ashore on the Atlantides Island. Orpheus begged them not to spurn the solemnities of the island, nor the secrets, the laws, customs, the religious rites and works...").

The contradictions between the story of Atlantis and that of Troy simply cannot be reconciled. As much as I value other works of Eberhard Zangger, in this instance he is chasing a phantom. In Plato's Atlantis account, mention is also made of a very special type of metal, that could only be found on Atlantis: "gold-copper ore" or orichalcum, which was "second only to gold" (Critias). Why then is there no mention of this unique alloy in Homer's descriptions? Or in Pliny? In Strabo? In Herodotus and the other historians? Because it did not exist in ancient Greece, neither in Troy nor elsewhere. Troy was not Atlantis. I know of only one country where such an alloy was found: in Peru, long before the Incas. The Indian cultures of Peru and Ecuador had mastered refined methods for making metal alloys and compounds, which were later forgotten. Their layering techniques were of such perfection that experts today shake their heads in wonder. The finest layers of copper, silver and gold have been discovered which, according to their composition, look like brighter or darker gold. Even acid tests on their surfaces do not reveal the composition of the mixtures. The goldsmiths of these Indian peoples must have known of a very ancient technology, by means of which they could "endow non-precious metals with the appearance of precious ones."[23] How did it go in the Atlantis story? "It was called orichalcum or "gold-copper ore" and next to gold was most prized by this ancient race."

In Plato's Atlantis story there is a staggering passage, which has been either overlooked or hardly mentioned by countless researchers. Assuming that Plato was right and this strange Atlantis island was situated in the Atlantic Ocean, then beyond this Atlantis (seen from Europe) would lie another country: America. What does Plato say?

> The travellers of those days could pass from this island to other islands, and from there reach the whole continent which lay on the other side of this sea...this realm [Atlantis] held sway over all the islands and many others, and a part of the mainland beyond.

If Plato had invented the whole dialogue, how would he have known about another mainland and continent that lay further west from Atlantis? In addition he clearly distinguishes here between "islands" and "mainland." So let's not waste time worrying about whether the Egyptians thought all foreigners came from "islands," and the theory that the dialogue is simply based on Plato's wish for an "ideal state." What we have here, as lawyers might say, are solid facts. But if Plato did not invent the whole thing, and the story came from Egypt, how did the Egyptians know about the American continent? They themselves say how: for more than

10,000 years they had kept careful written records, and in comparison to them the Greeks, who could only remember back to the most recent devastation, were like children. Since Columbus we too know about the continent beyond Atlantis. But Plato could not have known about it.

In the end I am less concerned with joining in the literary speculations about where Atlantis was, than in asking when it was, and how an island kingdom of such power and greatness could simply disappear from the face of the earth. (For those readers who are interested in further theories about Atlantis and where it might have been located, please see the section in the back of this book.)

Chapter 6
Help for Plato

*Clever people can pretend to be stupid. The other way
'round is more difficult.*

—Kurt Tucholsky, 1890–1935

People have short memories. Most are only interested in today's news, in sport, and inevitable daily problems, and everything else is pointless. Our computer and television age brought information closer to people, but did not actually change them. They cherish their fixed opinions as they always have done, fall into line behind some ideology, religion, or other, and in particular give hardly a thought to the past, for nothing's going to change it after all.

The past is definitely passé. Yet we are the product of our past, as humanity is of its history. Whoever knows something about history can draw conclusions from it, perhaps avoid mistakes which others made in the past, and assess the future more clearly. This is true both for the individual and for society as a whole. Perhaps our heads are round so that thinking can change track occasionally. That's not much help if our heads are empty, of course, for those who know nothing tend to believe everything.

When something from the past doesn't suit us, we disregard it by saying "things were different then." Young people don't pay much attention to the old, for they "lived in different times." We view our present as a point of culmination of all the past, as the zenith of all knowledge and information. Unfortunately this is not really so, at least if we ignore what we can learn from the past. The mass suppression of past events renders us helpless when similar events arise anew.

In Plato's *Dialogues*, it is claimed again and again that the human race has passed through several annihilations. Atlantis is only supposed to have been one of these. Most people don't agree with this theory, particularly in intellectual circles. Atlantis? Devastation? Poppycock! I am of a different opinion, for Plato's accounts can be proved. Absolutely definitely.

On a September morning in 1985, Monsieur Henri Cosquer, who was working for a diving school in Cassis (east of Marseilles) dove down into the deep water of the Morgiou Gape. He wasn't looking for anything in particular, apart from a chance to enjoy the beauty of the underwater scene. Beside a small slippage of rocks 115 feet (35m) down, Henri Cosquer noticed a cave mouth and swam carefully inside. He soon realized that the cave led to an ascending underwater tunnel. But he did not feel like going any further. He only had limited time, oxygen for another half hour, and he had neither underwater lights nor cameras with him.

A few weeks later he dived again to the same place. This time he had his friends Marc and Bernard with him, and better equipment than on the first occasion. The men swam carefully through a 130-foot (40m) long corridor and arrived at last at the surface of an underwater lake. Their spotlights illumined an incredible sight: painted on the west wall of this undersea hall they recognized two horses. Bernard turned his spotlight on the roof and found a goat drawn in black charcoal which was covered in a layer of transparent calcite. The men waded out of the water, took off their flippers and tried the air in the underground caverns. It was aromatic and resinous, but fine for breathing. In the adjoining hall, which was even bigger than the first, their lights flitted over a whole painting gallery: bison, penguins, cats, antelopes, a seal, and even some geometric symbols.

Henri Cosquer showed his photos to several archaeologists. They were uninterested, remained skeptical, or even regarded the pictures as forgeries. It was not until six years later, on September 19, 1991, that a research ship of the French navy, the *Archdonaute*, anchored off Cape Morgiou, and 11 frogmen followed Henri Cosquer into the cave system. Eight experts waited on board the *Archeonaute*, among them two archaeologists. Special equipment was lowered into the depths to map the underground gallery, and even to bring small samples of the paintings to the surface. These were later tested by the carbon-14 dating method, and shown to be at least 18,440 years old.

What does all this have to do with the Atlantis tradition? It is quite simple: 18,440 years ago the surface of the Mediterranean was 115 feet (35m) lower than it is today. In those days the entrance to the underground caves was on land. The water-level has risen.

Also in the Mediterranean lies Malta, with its prehistoric temples and "cart ruts," that is, track-like furrows in the limestone. At two places these "ruts" lead straight down into the depths of the Mediterranean. Since the creators of these prehistoric ruts were not intelligent fish nor had divers' suits made of bronze with wooden air-pumps, the only possible conclusion is the same: the sea-level has risen.

Image 41: On the island of Malta these rail-like tracks run everywhere. Some of them vanish into the depths of the Mediterranean.

Image 42 and 43: Rail-like tracks in Malta.

Does this apply only to the Mediterranean? No, it can be demonstrated all over the world. On the Atlantic coast near the Breton village of Carnac there stand thousands of menhirs (from the Celtic *men* meaning large, and *hir* meaning stone), arranged in colonnades, so-called "alignments." Originally, there must have been more than 15,000 such menhirs. Archaeologists are still scratching their heads about their significance. One of these stone colonnades vanishes into the depths of the Gulf of Morbihan. And off the little island of Er'Lanic lies a great underwater stone circle, which can just be seen at low tide through a diving mask. What conclusion can we draw? The sea-level of the Atlantic has also risen. There are numerous other examples that could be cited.[1]

Image 44: At Carnac in French Brittany, a stone circle sinks into the Atlantic Ocean.

So the rise in the sea-level of the Mediterranean and the Atlantic cannot be disputed. And what about the Pacific Ocean?

The south coast of the Japanese island Okinawa is a paradise for divers, for there, in the clear blue waters of the Pacific, lie many shipwrecks from World War II. In March 1995, divers came across strange rectangular stone structures in just over 100 feet (32 m) of water, all overgrown with coral. To begin with, the divers were not sure whether these were natural rock or stones cut by human hands. After several Japanese newspapers had reported the underwater discovery, a full-scale treasure hunt began. Many finds turned up immediately. Off the coast of the island of Yonaguni (southwest of Okinawa), but also in the waters around the neighboring islands of Kerama and Aguni, were found broad stairways which led to squares. Cobbled streets, altar-shaped structures, carved monoliths, and even a small tower were located.

The Japanese archaeologist Masaaki Kimura, of the University of the Ryukyu Islands on Okinawa, wrote a much-admired book (unfortunately only obtainable in Japanese) about these phenomenal underwater finds. Our conclusion must once more be the same: the sea-level of the Pacific Ocean has also risen.

Buildings over which the sea has closed can also be found near Bimini (in the Caribbean) or near Ponape (in the Caroline group of islands in the Pacific). But even above the surface something is not quite right with our simplistic textbook models. On the eastern edge of Mexico City rises the pyramid of Cuicuilco, nowadays long since surrounded by the suburbs. It is a rounded cone-shape, and consists of three levels. The apex is flattened, and the whole structure was built from head-size stones. Three sides of the pyramid were once engulfed in the lava and ash of a volcanic eruption. The layer of volcanic material is from 3 to 10 feet (1 to 3m) deep. Now logically the pyramid must have existed before it was covered by lava. Geologists think that the nearby volcano last erupted 7,000 or 8,000 years ago.

That is impossible, object the archaeologists. The cone pyramid of Cuicuilco must have been built between AD 500 and 800. There would be no sense in an earlier dating, because in Mexico 7,000 years ago there was no civilization capable of building such a pyramid. To resolve the dispute between geologists and archaeologists, small holes were drilled into the volcanic layer for 330 yards (300m) alongside the pyramid, and samples taken. All the samples contained charcoal and could therefore easily be dated using carbon-14 dating. This was carried out in 1957 and 1962 by the Radio-Carbon Laboratory of California University (UCLA) in

Los Angeles.² The 19 samples gave astonishingly varied results, varying between AD 414 and 4765 BC. So everyone was free to endorse the date that fit in with his own theory.

But mistakes were made when the samples were taken. Commissioned by the Mexican Direccion de Antropologia, the American archaeologist Dr. Byron Cummings had, in 1920, excavated parts of the pyramid deep into the ground. In doing so, he had opened three layers of volcanic material, and between each layer the remains of a different civilization had been clearly revealed. The three layers of lava and volcanic ash proved to be sterile, but in between—as though in a sandwich—bones, remains, and broken pieces of ceramic appeared. And there was evidence that the pyramid wall went down to the deepest layer. Dr. Cummings thought that the pyramid had first been built and then engulfed by the volcanic eruption; then another civilization had left its traces beside the pyramid until the volcano became active once more. This drama was repeated three times, and each time the pyramid was affected.³

Cuicuilco is only one example among many which have come to light in recent years, and which have been suppressed by classical archaeology.⁴,⁵ Many of the worthy men and women who belong to the archaeology fraternity don't even know about the new discoveries and false datings. Yet for the last 50 years at least, a document has been available for public scrutiny which, without any shadow of a doubt, gives proof of the existence of an advanced civilization more than 12,000 years ago. This was a civilization that drew maps, very precise ones too, both of the coastline of Antarctica and the islands off it—an Antarctica that was free of ice! The Antarctic continent, of course, has been hidden under a thick armor of ice for as long as human beings can remember. Here is the incredible story.

In 1929 the Topkapi palace in Istanbul was transformed into a museum of ancient artifacts. During the clearance work, a fragment of an old map fell into the hands of Halil Eldem, the director of the Turkish National Museum. The map had been drawn by Piri Reis, an admiral of the Ottoman fleet (see picture 39). Piri Reis had begun it in 1513, but did not hand his completed work to Sultan Selim I until four years later. The map, now known as the Piri Reis map, was painted on gazelle hide in delicate colors.

Piri Reis had added handwritten remarks to the left edge of the map. As well as being in charge of the fleet, he was also deeply interested in the maritime sciences of his day. He is also the author of a booklet entitled *Bahriye*, in which he refers to various aspects of his map and explains how he created it. Towns and castles are marked with red lines, uninhabited regions with black lines, cliffs and rocky areas with black dots, sandy spots with red dots, and hidden reefs with crosses. Piri Reis also explains that he composed this map from 20 different older maps, and even used a map by Christopher Columbus. This would have been possible, for the discoverer of America had come back to Europe in 1500 before his third voyage. In the Mediterranean of those days, there were frequent pirate attacks and conflicts between various neighboring nations. It might well have happened that a Portuguese or Spanish ship fell into the hands of the Turks. Piri Reis says he also used maps which had come from the time of Alexander the Great (died 323 BC), and still others which were based on geometric tables. It was clear that the Turkish admiral was well aware of the uniqueness of his map, for he also wrote, "No one owns a map like this at present!"

People very soon noticed that Piri Reis's handiwork only covered half the world; the gazelle hide was torn, so that the right side of the map was missing. Soon after its discovery, the German Orientalist Professor Kahle turned his attention to it, and in September 1931 at the 18th Orientalist Congress in the Dutch town of Leiden, he announced that Piri Reis must have used parts of a lost Columbus map.[6] In the autumn of 1931, Professor Oberhammer, at that time also a member of the Vienna Academy of Science, examined this unusual object, and came to the same conclusion as his colleague Kahle.

A number of newspapers reported on the Piri Reis map, after which the "society for research into Turkish history" commissioned the state printing works in Istanbul to make the map available to a wider circle of scholars. In 1933, therefore, the map was transposed on to a metal printing plate and reproduced in a facsimile edition of 1,000 copies. The first edition ran out within a few months, so the supreme command of the Turkish navy (the Hydrographic Institute) commissioned a new print-run. This time, 12,500 copies of the maps were printed in full-size format, and 10,000 copies in a reduced size.

In the 1940s, copies of the Piri Reis map were bought by many museums and libraries. In 1954, a copy reached the desk of the American cartographer Arlington H. Mallery, who had specialized in old sea maps for decades. The Piri Reis map electrified Mallery, for at its lower edge was a continent with offshore islands, of which Piri Reis could have known nothing in 1513. This was Antarctica. Even if the Turk had used a map drawn by Christopher Columbus, this did not solve the riddle, for he too had known nothing of Antarctica.

Arlington Mallery asked his colleague, Walters, of the U.S. Navy's Hydrographic Institute, for his opinion about the map. Walters was baffled. He was particularly astonished by the exactness of the distance between the Old and New Worlds. In 1513, when Piri Reis drew his map, America had not yet featured on any map, and even one drawn by Columbus could never have contained so many precise details. Even outlying areas, such as the high mountainous terrain in western South America, were reproduced— in other words regions which, as far as we know, were first explored by Francisco Pizarro (1478–1541). Equally baffling was the precise position of the Canary Islands or the Azores. The two cartographers also soon noticed that Piri Reis had either rejected the coordinates usual at the time, or had viewed the earth as a flat disc. In order to get a clear picture, Mallery and Walters placed a coordinate grid over the map, in order to transfer individual positions to a globe.

Now their astonishment was complete. Not only the contours of North and South America, but also Antarctica's coastline, were positioned exactly where we would expect to find them today. But where a stormy sea now rages south of Terra del Fuego, there was a narrow bridge of land to Antarctica. Inch for inch they compared the Piri Reis map with land profiles which had been obtained by means of the most modern technology, both from the air and from echo-soundings at sea. Toward the end of the last Ice Age, about 12,000 years ago, there had indeed been a land-bridge at this selfsame place. In the southern polar region, Piri Reis had mapped the coastline and its bays with painstaking accuracy, as well as the offshore islands. "No one can see these coastlines and islands today, for they are covered by a thick sheet of ice."[7]

It was no different in Piri Reis' day, so where did he get his information from?

During the International Year of Geophysics in 1957, the Jesuit Father Lineham, who was then director of Weston Observatory and a cartographer for the U.S. Navy, examined the Piri Reis map. He came to the same conclusion as his colleagues. The Antarctic part demonstrated an incredible accuracy, with many details which had only become generally known following the Swedish–British–Norwegian expeditions of 1949 and 1952. On August 28, 1958, the University of Georgetown organized a public hearing about the mystery of the Piri Reis map. Let me quote some excerpts from it:

Walters: It is difficult for us to understand nowadays how cartographers could have been so accurate many centuries before us, since it is only recently that we invented the modern, scientific method of cartography.

Mallery: This was, of course, a problem which we scratched our heads over. We could not imagine how such a precise map could have been made without airplanes. But the fact remains that they made it. And not only that: they got the longitude measurements absolutely right, something we have only been able to do in the last 200 years.

Walters: Father Lineham, you were involved in seismological research into Antarctica. Do you share the enthusiasm about these new discoveries?

Lineham: Certainly I do. With the seismological method we have discovered things which seem to confirm a great many of the drawings reproduced on the map: the land masses, the projection of mountains, seas, islands.... I think the seismological method will allow us to remove, as it were, more of the ice-layer from the regions depicted on the [Piri Reis] map, and this will show that this map is even more accurate than we are at the moment prepared to accept.[8]

After the American academic press had reported on the map, it also came to the attention of Charles Hapgood, a professor of history at Keene State University in New Hampshire. He got hold of a copy and began to analyze it thoroughly, together with his students. The results of this joint work took the form of a scientific publication, whose conclusions are revealed in its foreword:

> This book contains the history of the discovery of the first solid proof that an advanced people was far superior to all other human groups of which history tells us.... It seems incredible, but the proofs show quite clearly that some ancient people or other mapped the coastline of Antarctica at a time when its coasts were free of ice. It is equally clear that this people must have had access to navigational instruments in order to determine longitude in a way which was far superior to anything we knew of until the middle of the 18th century. Until now scholars have dismissed such claims as myth, but here before us are the indisputable proofs.[9]

On July 6, 1960, Harold Z. Ohlmeyer, then head of the U.S. Air Force Department, which was involved in mapping Antarctica, wrote to Professor Charles Hapgood:

> The coastline [on the Piri Reis map] must have been mapped before the Antarctic was covered in ice. The ice in this region is nowadays roughly a mile thick. We have absolutely no idea how the data on the Piri Reis map can be reconciled with the geographic knowledge of 1513.[10]

Professor Hapgood and his students worked on the Piri Reis map for two years. What grid of coordinates had the Turk used? Where was the reference point for these coordinates? It soon became clear that this had to be in Egypt, in Alexandria to be precise. Now Piri Reis had obviously taken account of the globe-shape of the earth—but how? It turned out that he must have used a system of trigonometry (triangulation). But where did he get this from?

The Greek Eratosthenes (died 275 BC) was a known map-maker of antiquity. He had even been director of the Alexandria library under

Ptolemy III. He also wrote three books about cartographic measurements (*Geographika*). But it was clear that Eratosthenes had not used trigonometry in his maps. Professor Hapgood and his students were soon convinced that the map-maker responsible for the original upon which Piri Reis drew, "had access to a more advanced science than the ancient Greeks."[11] The maps and documents which the Turk used must come from scientific sources that were active in a far-distant past.

Professor Hapgood and his team were soon able to draw up precise comparative tables between the Piri Reis map and modem maps. The discrepancies are small, and in many cases practically non-existent. This is quite astonishing. How on earth can the coastlines of Antarctica, together with its offshore islands, which have lain under an armor plating of ice for millennia, come to be on an old map? And so accurately that comparison with the most up-to-date maps reveals hardly any, or even, in many places, no discrepancy? A miracle? But miracles have some basis in fact.

And yet in spite of all its accuracy there is something wrong with the Piri Reis map, which nothing could really explain. Hapgood said of this: "Parts of the Caribbean on the Piri Reis map presented us with the greatest difficulties. They don't seem to fit in to the rest of the picture."[12] The map shows only the eastern coast of Cuba. The whole western side is missing. Instead, something is attached to the western side that cannot be Cuba, and yet is twice as big as the Caribbean islands of today. Hapgood said of this: "Strange to say there exists on the Piri Reis map a complete, western coastline where this island is in reality truncated."[13] It is obvious that Piri Reis had problems with Cuba, for he also gave the island the wrong name: Espaniola. Columbus did not name Cuba "Espaniola," but called its neighboring islands, Haiti and the Dominican Republic, "Hispaniola." How did this glaring mistake find its way in to the otherwise perfect map? Professor Hapgood suspects that Piri Reis used a very ancient map on which Cuba was drawn differently than it is today, but that he also had a Columbus map, or—as Piri Reis says in his book *Bahriye*—he asked a sailor who had taken part in Columbus voyage of discovery. The mistake with Cuba could have arisen through confusion between the Columbus map (and/or the conversation with the sailor) on the one hand, and the old map from an unknown source on the other.

That may be true. But what did the original, ancient map—which might well have come from the library at Alexandria—have in the place of Cuba? How does someone like Piri Reis come to make such a mess of the Caribbean island of Cuba, yet get the coastline of Antarctica so exact? Something else, probably a large island, must no doubt have been on the unknown original. Could it have been Atlantis?

Our current state of knowledge is unable to answer this. A few indications, though, can give us pause for thought. Columbus named his newly-discovered land "Hispaniola," but the native Indians called it "Quisqueya" or "Mother of Lands."[14] Was this a reference to ancient tradition? In the Greek version of the Atlantis legend, Plato calls it "Polis Atlantis" or "City of Atlas."

Strangely enough, this same name appears in several stories from Central America. That mysterious realm of Tula, which the Mayans speak of, was once called "Izmachi" and still longer ago Aztlan'. Joachim Rittstig, former principal of the German School in El Salvador, and expert in the Mayan calendar, wrote a booklet which made astonishing links between Atlantis and the Indian cultures of Central America.[15] According to his research, it can be clearly seen from Mayan texts that there was a city named Aztlan in 12901 BC, in what is now Guatemala. It is even given an exact geographical location: 15° 33-5' North; 890° 05.5' West. I am not in a position to judge whether Rittstig's conclusions are right in all respects, and I also know that there were not yet any Mayans around in 12901 BC. But that is not the end of the matter: tribes change their names, and sometimes carry with them memories of traditions which are millennia old.

In the (later) Mayan cities, sculptures were made which are still cause for wonder, and which no Mayan expert understands. Some prime examples of these stand in the ancient Mayan metropolis of Copan in Honduras. The more one looks at these curious steles and "anthropomorphic structures," the more one thinks of an ur-ancient, technical civilization. These figures were no doubt immortalized in stone by a society which had long forgotten how such technical mysteries once functioned. The important thing was that they were connected to the gods. Even the carving on the world-famous grave-slab of Palenque (Mexico), which experts believe belonged to the Mayan ruler Pacal, belongs to this type. The view of various students of ancient America that such representations are of ominous "cosmic monsters"[16] has no helpful or sensible bearing on the grave-stone of Palenque.[17]

We really shouldn't forget that even the well-known word "Aztec" comes from "Aztlan." The "people of Aztlan," the forefathers of the Aztecs, are said to have originally lived on an island.[18] And the Spanish monk Fray Diego Durin writes in his *History of the Indian Lands of New Spain* that the tribes are said to have taken refuge in the caves of "Aztlan and Tecolhuacan" after a terrible catastrophe. Their original homeland had been Aztlan.[19]

Although I don't want to go searching for Atlantis, I wouldn't mind betting that it lay somewhere in the Caribbean region. Plato certainly started something with his Atlantis story. Around about 3,600 books have been written about it.[20] This seemingly endless theme stimulates much debate and excites a lot of interest. No doubt people will speculate about where Atlantis was until it is located, but there is one thing which is quite certain from a geological perspective. Atlantis cannot have "gone under," in the sense of simply sinking under the waves. The geologist Dr. Johannes Fiebag explains why:

> A comparison between the sea-floor and the land reveals a fundamental difference between them. The sea-floor is generally composed of very flat plates, while the continents in contrast are vast blocks which float on the so-called asthenosphere. Wherever a subduction zone can be observed in the border region between continent and ocean, one finds that the sea-floor sinks below the continent. This is because the sea-floor consists mainly of basalt, while the continents are generally of granite material and sediment. Basalt has a higher specific weight than gravity, which is why the heavier ocean plates always sink down and the continents, floating like an iceberg on the water in the asthenosphere, never do.

This would be absolutely, physically impossible. A continent like Atlantis *cannot* sink. It is prevented from doing so by its specific weight.[21]

In spite of this clear, scientific perspective, Atlantis has vanished from the face of the earth, "sunk into the depths" as Plato said. Now a land does not have to sink for the waves to cover it—this can occur when the sea-level rises. And no one disputes that this is what happened when the glaciers melted at the end of the last Ice Age. But the rise in sea-level took place slowly, and not "in a single terrible night" (Plato). The technically advanced inhabitants of Atlantis would have been able to save themselves in good time by taking to ships—unless of course a cosmic catastrophe had compounded the one caused by melting ice; or unless such a catastrophe, perhaps an asteroid hitting the earth, had started an immense tidal wave, which in turn had led to the ice melting. Nowadays we have data that clearly confirms that some huge catastrophe must have happened in mankind's past.

- Geologists discovered ocean corals on Hawaii at a height of 1,000 feet (300m), which must have been deposited there by a tidal wave.[22]

- Around 11,400 years ago, temperatures on earth rose by 7 degrees within one decade: "In 1993 samples taken from drillings into Greenland ice revealed, surprisingly, that the Ice Age did not gradually fade out, but ended suddenly."[23]

- In the past 67 years, astronomers have discovered a total of 108 small planets which have passed close to the earth. One of these, named XFII, will come within a mere million miles on October 26, 2028. Any impact of an asteroid on the surface of the ocean would cause a tidal wave. "Several thousand kilometers of coastline would be flooded, innumerable cities would be transformed into muddy devastation."[24]

I live in a generation which regards a possible climatic catastrophe as a serious possibility. The so-called "greenhouse effect" is meant to spread over the globe and bring about a rise in temperatures. Man is to blame for this, for he produces the dangerous carbon dioxide gas (CO_2). Whoever does not go along with this view of impending doom is held to be irresponsible and unreasonable. Never mind that 81 percent of all American climatologists view the greenhouse effect in a quite different way, based on convincing data. The world of ideological misinformation carries on regardless. Computers are fed false data "which is based on obscure simulation models."[25] Fairly little of what climate researchers deign to tell us is accurate. Too many of these environmentalists work according to the principle of "mega-garbage in, mega-garbage out."

And they are even paid well for doing it. Everything is possible in politics!

These people are clearly lacking in historical awareness. No one can seriously dispute that northern Europe was shrouded in an Ice Age 10,000 years ago. There are lumps of stone lying around in the landscape to prove it—known in geology as "erratic blocks"—which arrived on the backs of glaciers. What was it that led then, and in many previous temperature changes, to abrupt rises in temperature, and subsequent Ice Ages?

Plato got it right. There were periodic devastations, particularly in coastal regions, either with or without human help. Now I am as concerned as the next man to make sure we keep our world clean. But I object to a paralyzing, "no-future" mentality; which through lack of knowledge of the earth's history invokes a drama of guilt, even of original sin. This is a drama, rather, that has already been played out many times, and not one caused by the politically correct flavor of the moment.

The sea-level *did* rise, and catastrophes *did* occur. We have a Piri Reis map with an ice-free Antarctic to prove it. And off Okinawa Island in Japan lie ancient structures under the water. You may also have heard that the Sahara was once a fertile garden—and it doesn't really matter which witness I call on to support the claim: whether the Greek geographer Strabo (roughly 62 BC to AD 26); the Roman historian Gaius Plinius Caecilius Secundus (AD 61–113); the Greeks Hesiod, Herodotus or Hecataios (550–480 BC); Diodorus of Sicily (1st century BC); or the more ancient Phoenician Sanchuniathon (about 1250 BC). Whether I quote the Bible's 10 antediluvian patriarchs or the ancient Babylonian list of kings, or ancient Indian and Tibetan texts, it all comes to the same thing in the end. All of them give accounts of events which occurred 10,000 years and more ago. I noted in the Preface that this book was not about Greek history but about Greek stories. These stories are evidently much older than the research sets out, although they cannot at present be dated. But many of the events described are connected in some way with high technology in antiquity. Apollo's flying chariot or the robot Talos, patrolling Crete, are just two examples. But high technology in antiquity does not sit well with the people of the Stone Age. Hence my case: the gods were alien astronauts.

The fact that our science, which also influences the media, wishes to know nothing about all this, is simply a sign of its failings. But there isn't much point in getting overheated about it in one's own little greenhouse. As Marcus Aurelius, a Roman Caesar once said, "It is senseless to get annoyed with the world, for it isn't in the least bit bothered if you do."

A Final Word on Atlantis

A number of years have passed since I wrote the manuscript for *Odyssey of the Gods*. But the flow of information has not abated. Almost on a monthly basis, texts from ancient books land on my desk, books which have been available for hundreds of years, whose content may go back millennia, which someone at some point has decided to translate. But these ancient translations are not a monolithic block. In contrast to the exact sciences, the information-gathering sciences are alive and adapt to new findings. Information gathering sciences, in which indicators are put in order and words are weighed, are not dogmatic. Science is alive. Time never stands still.

Where actually did Atlantis lie? As long ago as 1954, L. Sprague de Camps in his book *Lost Continents*[1] presented a list of 50 locations where various researchers assumed Atlantis to be. They included North Africa, Ceylon, Mongolia, Spitsbergen, Carthage, Cadez (the old name for Cadiz), the Atlas mountains, Tartessos (Spain), South Africa, Tunisia, Malta, central France, the Caucasus, the western Mediterranean, the North Sea, the Sahara, East Prussia, the Baltic, the Ahaggar mountains (Algeria), Greenland, Iran, Central America, Iraq, the Crimea, the West Indies, Belgium, Holland, Sweden, Catalonia, the British Isles, the Arctic, a continent in the Pacific, Australia, and southern India. And since 1954, Crete, Bimini, Santorini, the Azores, the southern tip of Japan and, the most recent location, Troy have been added.

Until some dive boat photographs the ruins of Atlantis, it remains meaningless to speculate about its geographical location. Every researcher can come up with reasonable grounds why Atlantis should lie in his favored location. And yet no one has found it.

As I made clear in this book, I take Plato's description seriously. Atlantis *did* exist. But, *when?*

Plato assures us that the Egyptians saved all the information from ancient times in written documents in their temples and preserved it from destruction.[2] According to these temple records, a war had taken place between Atlantis and the mainland, and this had been 9,000 years ago. If we add on the time from Plato to the present day, that would come to more or less 11,400 years. Strange, because the classical Greek historiographer Herodotus refers to similar figures. He is also called the "father of historiography." In the second book of his *Histories,* Herodotus recounts his visit to Thebes (the present-day Luxor). The priests had shown him 341 statues with a brief explanation for each. These 341 statues correspond to 11,340 years. In the time preceding these 11,340 years, the gods had resided on earth, and "since that time there has been no god in human form in Egypt any more.... The Egyptians are very certain of that because they continuously calculated and recorded the periods of the kings and high priests."[3]

Why are there no written records from that time, which lies more than 10,000 years in the past? Look it up in Plato (my emphasis in italics):

"The reason is as follows: the destructions which are and will be visited upon humanity are numerous and of many different kinds, the mightiest of them through fire and water, other smaller ones through innumerable other causes. Because the story you, too, tell, that a long time ago Phaethon, the son of Helios, took control of his father's chariot but, incapable of keeping to his father's path, destroyed wide swathes of land through fire and was himself killed by a lightning bolt—that may sound like a fairy tale, *but in truth it represents a deviation of the heavenly bodies revolving around the earth and a cataclysm on the earth's surface through a great conflagration, recurring after long intervals of time.*"

If Plato is right, there must have been a planetary catastrophe in our solar system x-thousand years ago. *"A deviation of the heavenly bodies revolving around the earth..."* How did anyone know anything about the planetary orbits 2,400 years ago? In the 17th century, Galileo Galilei was to be put to death because of what he said about the planets. That is what the Inquisition wanted. But all the things taught by Galileo could already be found in Plato. Furthermore, a planetary catastrophe would have affected other peoples on earth. After all, the earth is a sphere which revolves around its own axis once every 24 hours. Are there records of that anywhere else outside the Mediterranean area?

During and after the Spanish conquests, the so-called *Books of Chilam Balam* were written in Central America. *Chilam* means "prophet" or "interpreter of the gods"; *balam* means "jaguar." These books are distinguished from one another by adding the name of the place where they are kept. Thus there is a Chilam Balam book of Mani, one of Balam, others of Chumayel, Ixil, Tekax, and so on. The books, written in Latin script but using the Yucatec language, were created between the 16th and 18th centuries. The content was compiled by many priests and written by different hands. The whole thing is a mixture of ancient stories and abstruse prophecies—a read which is often difficult to understand composed almost 500 years ago. The sources, on the other hand, from which the priests obtained their information were very ancient. These original sources are missing quite simply for the reason that the Spanish destroyed all Mayan manuscripts (except for three of which two are almost indecipherable). We might well ask whether there is anything that 500-year-old books can still tell us about the origin of humanity and the gods. I know Muslims who can recite the Koran sura by sura. I have met Christians who know the New Testament by heart, and Jews who can immediately recall the Torah (the Pentateuch with the Five Books of Moses) from memory. Many faithful know the essential content of their religions—even if not word for word off by heart. If a terrible war turned all Bibles to dust and ashes but a number of priests and pious lay people survived, the holy scriptures could be reconstructed from memory and written down again. The same thing happened in the Central America of the 16th century. Priests and tribal elders collected memories and traditional narratives from the time of the gods. Only the paper on which they were written down was new. The creation of the earth is set out in the *Chilam Balam Book* of Chumayel thus:

This is the history of the world as it was written down in ancient days, because the time has not yet passed for making books like this...so that the Mayan peoples may learn how they were born in this country.... It happened in Katun 11 Ahau (date), when Ah Muzencab (descending god) appeared. It was the time when fire descended, then the rope fell down, followed by the rocks and trees....[4]

The *Chilam Balam Book* of Mani even mentions the descent of those gods: "This is the report about the descent of one god, the 13 gods, and the one thousand gods, who instructed the priests Chilam Balam, Xupan, Nauat..."[5]

Besides these *Chilam Balam Books*, there are also ancient Mexican manuscripts in Central America. A medley of texts with many pictures ferreted out by the clever Abbé Brasseur de Bourgbourg. This Abbé Brasseur was a genius at languages. He had learned Aztec in Mexico and was able to decipher the ancient manuscripts with the help of Aztec priests. Brasseur named one of these manuscripts after his Indian teacher, Chimalpopoca. Hence the text is called *Codex Chimalpopoca*.[6] According to the codex, the gods first created heaven and earth, then the fire drill fell down. This having been done, the gods considered which of them should in future live on earth: "Sorrowfully it is pondered by the one with the garment of stars, the wealthy of stars, the mistress in the water, the one who comes over people, stamps on the earth, Quetzalcoatl."[7]

The same codex also states that the sun only became visible in the fifth eon, and in this eon "was created the earth, heaven and the four types of human inhabitants." It has not been possible to discover from whence the ancient Mexicans knew anything about the four types of human inhabitants.

A spectral great fire and the sun darkening into eerie night are described in dramatic terms: "The second sun had been created. Four Jaguar was its day sign. It is called January sun. It came about that the heavens fell in and the sun did not at that time follow its path. Midday had just come, immediately it turned to night."[8]

What did this refer to? A geomagnetic reversal? An abrupt shift in the earth's axis? This incomprehensible spectacle turned into a global catastrophe in the eon of the third sun:

> It is called fire rain sun. In this eon it happened that it rained fire and its inhabitants were burned up.... The ancients tell that at that time the rocky sands were scattered which we see now, and the blistered andesitic lavas bubbled up, and at that time the various reddish rocks were deposited.[9]

What is being written about here?

As everyone knows, there is an unnatural gap between Mars and Jupiter which contains thousands of asteroids. The origin of this asteroid belt is a controversial subject to the present day. One of the theories says that the debris has come from an exploded planet. The description in the Codex Chimalpopoca would fit this theory very well. The explosion of a planet in our solar system would obscure the sun for months or, indeed, years. Cosmic dust would travel through the solar system, red hot debris hit the earth. White hot bombs would shred the thin, delicate skin of our planet, shake it and rock it—not just through such cosmic missiles but also through the shift of the gravitational forces in the solar system. The exploded planet would cause an imbalance in the complex structure of our planetary orbits. Floods, an obscured sun, and a rain of fire would be the logical consequence. To inhabitants on earth, it must seem as if the heavens are on fire and falling in on them. All the elements would be raging, the oceans pouring over the land, hurricanes whipping up the water masses, and volcanoes erupting everywhere.

Was this what was recounted in the Codex Chimalpopoca *and* in Plato? The continuation of this drama is described in the *Popol Vuh*, the holy book of the Quiché Maya.[10] There we can read how human beings strayed aimlessly about and arduously sought refuge from the forces which had been unleashed. Close to starvation, increasing numbers of Indians gathered on the summit of the mountain Hacawitz—also called "resting place." Freezing they stood in the endless night, cowering by the images of their gods, not understanding what had happened:

Sleep was not for them, nor rest. Great was their lamentation in their innermost heart that daybreak failed to come and it refused to become light. Their only expression was one of despondency, great sadness, and dejection overcame them; they were wholly bewildered by pain.... Oh, if only they could see the birth of the sun, they said, and talked much among themselves.... And then the sun rose. And little animals and big animals were overjoyed, all of them standing at the riverbeds and the ravines; and those who were on the summits of the mountains together turned their gaze to where the sun was rising....[11]

The Mayan kingdom is calculated on a generous timescale to have existed from 1500 BC to AD 1600. But during this time there were no global catastrophes. The Egyptians, Babylonians, Greeks, and Romans, too, would have reported about it. In the last 3,000 years, the sun has not darkened, the heavens have not burned, no flood has destroyed the face of the earth, no "gods" have descended from the firmament. So it must be assumed that the chronicles of the Central American Indians describe events which took place *before* their own time. No difference to Plato's report on the other side of the earth.

The Mayans coined the term "new world" for the period which started after the destruction. In this "new world," astronomy continued to be considered to be preeminent among the sciences. The Mayans were absolutely obsessed with it. In this context, all observation of the heavens appears to have fallen into two categories: 1) changes and movements in the firmament, and 2) cosmic catastrophes. This is confirmed by the missionary and cultural researcher Bernardino de Sahagun (1500–1590). This Franciscan monk not only undertook research into the language of the Aztecs but also of the Nahua. This group of Indian peoples already existed at the time of the Toltecs—around 100 BC. Their language, Nahuatl, was spoken by most of the rural population at the time of Bernardino de Sahagun. Now Bernardino de Sahagun was the head of the College of Santa Cruz on the Caribbean coast which was visited by many of the indigenous people. Sahagun sat down with them for weeks on end, cultivated their friendship, and asked them to tell him what they knew about the past of their tribes.

He recorded the results in the *Historia General de las Cosas de Nueva España*[12] (General History of the Things of New Spain). In it the indigenous people describe their fears of the celestial phenomena:

> When night came, everyone was very afraid, people expected that, as they said, the fire drill would not fall down properly. Then everyone would be destroyed, the end would have come, it would become night for ever. The sun would no longer rise so that it would become completely dark. Tzitzitzimi monsters would come falling down and destroy human beings...and no one lay down on the ground, it was said, but people climbed on their flat roofs. That is the extent to which everyone was caught up in magical belief that one should beware of the heavens, of the stars whose name is 'the many' and 'the fire drill.'[13]

The *Historia* also refers to "smoking stars," although it is not clear whether the reference is to meteorites or shooting stars. And when the sun disappeared even some of the gods were perturbed when they looked on the firmament: "As it was said, those who looked there were Quetzalcoatl, also called Ecatl, then Totec, or the lord of the ring, furthermore the red Tezcatlipoca. Then those who call themselves cloud snakes."[14]

The names of the Mayan and Aztec gods in Central America sound completely different from those in ancient Egypt or ancient Greece. Yet the *content* of the ancient records is similar in many respects. (In order to spare the reader unnecessary repetition, I refer to my last two books *History Is Wrong* and *Twilight of the Gods*.[15, 16])

Besides the Piri Reis map, besides Herodotus' number of 11,340 years, besides Plato's remark of 9,000 years *before* our time (today 11,400 years), besides the gods enthroned in the heavens—both in Central America, in Greece and in Egypt—there are additional links. The archeologist Otto Muck as long as 35 years ago pointed out common linguistic roots both in Central America and in Spain:

> The Basques still live in Spain and south-western France today. Plato expressly states that this part of Europe belonged to the Atlantean kingdom. The Basques were the closest neighbors of

Atlantis on European soil of which there are still ethnic groups remaining.... One of these reasons is provided by the Basques themselves. They still have a clear, express memory—of Atlantis.[17]

Muck points out that the Basques even today still possess the same facial features with the eagle nose as the Mayans in Mexico. They still wear similar clothing today, use the same knives and cultivate their fields in the same way. Curiously, both in the Basque country and in Mayan lands there are more than a hundred words with the same roots and meaning.

The geographical location of Atlantis has not yet been unambiguously found. But all the indications are that Atlantis existed. And both Plato and the ancient Central American books mention a planetary catastrophe which happened sometime 11,400 years ago. At that time the gods lived among human beings—according to Herodotus. And like all ancient cultures, the Mayans were also longingly awaiting the return of these gods, as recorded in the *Chilam Balam Book of Tizimin*:

> They came down from the avenue of the stars...they spoke the magical language of the stars in the heavens....Yes, their sign is our certainty that they came from the heavens...and when they come down from the heavens again they will create new order among their creation of long ago.[18]

There is something else that confuses me. Plato writes about a special metal—orichalcum—which was only and exclusively used in Atlantis. The special alloy of this orichalcum came directly from one of the sons of the gods, Poseidon. Orichalcum glistened like gold, was very thin, and was most similar to gold. Metal sheets have indeed been found with a very strange, paper-thin gold alloy in the highlands of Ecuador/South America.

There, in the city of Cuenca, there is a church called *Maria Auxiliadora* ("helpful Mother of God"). For more than 50 years, Father Carlo Crespi looked after the Catholic congregation. The Father enjoyed the reputation of a reliable friend of the indigenous people, and even during his lifetime, the people of Cuenca considered him a saint. Father Crespi has meanwhile died. The inhabitants built a memorial to him which every day has fresh flowers placed on it to the present day. What was so special about this

Father? He listened to the indigenous people, for days on end. He won their trust and helped them in every conceivable way.

The indigenous people returned the compliment and gave the good-hearted priest ancient works of art which their families had kept hidden from the whites for centuries. They were metal sheets which looked as if they were pure gold. Father Crespi began by placing these works of art against the walls of a locked inner courtyard, but as their number grew he stacked them on top of one another in two rooms. I visited him several times in the 1970s and photographed hundreds of these strange objects. These metal sheets tell continuing picture stories. The compositions are superimposed over one another. Faces crowned by the sun, heads with radiating beams, pyramids with indecipherable characters, people in some kind of "chainmail coat." Then there are rectangular steles made of metal with characters engraved on them which no one can decipher. In all, the steles have 14 lines with four squares in each line and a character in each square—a total of 56 squares with 56 characters.

The alloys on these metal plates have been thoroughly examined by scientists at the Max Planck Institute for Metals Research in Stuttgart. The result revealed an incredible smelting technique. They mixed 50 percent copper with 25 percent silver and 25 percent gold. Prof. Dr. Gebhardt from the Max Planck Institute in Stuttgart wrote to me:

> The pre-Inca tribes were capable of incredible methods of smelting and creating alloys which have never been surpassed. The external color of the object says nothing whatsoever about the percentage of gold. The same is true of the weight. The pre-Incas were capable of gold coatings which were only half a micrometer thick and which can only be seen, even with microscope, at a magnification of 500.[19]

The same was confirmed by Dr. Heather Lechtman, director of the Center for Materials Research in Archaeology and Ethnology at the Massachusetts Institute of Technology. She undertook a lengthy study of the "false Inca gold." The following sentences are taken from her research report:

We analyzed smaller samples of the artifacts in our laboratory. It
turned out that the coating in many places was only between about
0.5 to 2 micrometers thick and was hardly visible even under the
microscope with a magnification of up to 600.... Objects were used
which looked as if they were pure gold or silver.... The methods
of surface treatment used by the inhabitants of America in pre-
Columbian times to give base metals the appearance of precious
metals have never been surpassed.[20]

That is precisely what Plato says about the unique orichalcum alloy.

All our technology today is based on the past. It was our ancestors who
first discovered how metals can be extracted from the ground, how heavy
stones can be lifted, how ships, cars, aircraft, and washing machines can
be built. Everything is subject to the evolution of technology. There is no
technological evolution of orichalcum. The indigenous peoples should really have laboriously developed their sophisticated smelting and mixing
technologies. There should be precursors of these incredible alloys. There
should have been a learning process.

But there is no sign of any such thing. Orichalcum simply appeared. As
if a god had instructed human beings. As in Atlantis.

A Note to the Reader

If you have reached the end of this book, you may well be interested in the themes I deal with. If so, I would like to introduce you to the AASRS, or Archaeology, Astronautics, and SETI Research Society. SETI stands for the "Search for Extraterrestrial Intelligence." The AASRS collects and publishes information and ideas which support the theory that I have described in this book. Did extraterrestrials visit our planet millennia ago? How can a fascinating theory of this kind be proven? What speaks for it, and what against it?

The AASRS organizes conferences, gatherings, seminars, and field trips. I usually guide the tours myself. The AASRS publishes the fully illustrated magazine *Legendary Times* six times a year, in which you can find the latest contributions to our theme, as well as news of our activities. Membership of the AASRS is open to all. We are an organization of laypeople and scientists from all walks of life. If you would like to hear more, please send a postcard with your name and address to:

> AAS RA
> P.O. Box 6400
> Oceanside, CA 92052-6400, USA

Within four weeks you will receive a free brochure about the AASRS. Our internet address is *www.legendarytimes.com.*

—Erich von Daniken

Notes

Preface

1. *Der grosse Brockhaus* (Wiesbaden, 1953).
2. Josef Karst, *Eusebius Werke, 5. Band: die Chronik* (Leipzig 1911).

Chapter 1

1. Herbert Hunger, *Lexikon der griechischen und römischen Mythologie* (Vienna [no date given]).
2. Robert Graves, *The Greek Myths* (Penguin, 1993).
3. Gustav Schwab, *Sagen des klassischen Altertums* (Vienna and Heidelberg, 1972).
4. Ludwig Radermacher, *Mythos und Sage bei den Griechen* (Munich and Vienna, 1938).
5. Hermann Frankel, *Noten zu den Aeronautica des Apollonius* (Munich, 1963).
6. Paul Drager, *Argo Pasimelousa: Der Argonautenmythos in der griechischen und ramischen Literatur* (Stuttgart, 1993).
7. Jeffery S. Rusten, *Dionysius Scytobrachion* (Opladen, 1982).
8. Graves, *The Greek Myths.*
9. Georg Wissowa, *Paulys Realencyclopädie der Classischen Altertumswissenschaft* (Stuttgart, 1895).
10. Hunger, *Lexikon der griechischen und römischen Mythologie.*
11. George W. Mooney, *The Argonautica of Apollonius Rhodius* (Dublin, 1912).
12. Emile Delage and Vian, Francis, *Apollonius de Rhodes: Argonautiques, Tome III, Chant IV* (Paris, 1981).

13. Karl Schefold and Jung, Franz, *Die Sagen von den Argonauten, von Theben und Troja in der klassischen und hellenistischen Kunst* (Stuttgart, 1996).

14. This refers to the name of a town.

15. *Die Argonauten des Apollonius* (Zurich, 1779).

16. W.H. Roscher, *Ausführliches Lexikon der Griechischen und Römischen Mythologie* (Leipzig, 1890).

17. *Die Argonauten des Apollonius.*

18. Roscher, *Ausführliches Lexikon der Griechischen und Römischen Mythologie.*

19. Hubert Cancik and Schneider, Helmuth, *Der neue Pauly: Enzyklopädie der Antike* (Weimar [no date given]).

20. Edward Tripp (translator), *Reclams Lexikon der antiken Mythologie* (Stuttgart, 1994).

21. *Der grosse Brockhaus* (Wiesbaden, 1953).

22. *Die Argonauten des Apollonius.*

23. Genesis 6:4. *Die Heilige Schrift des Alten und des Neuen Testaments* (Stuttgart, 1972).

24. Paul Riessler, *Altjüdisches Schrifttum ausserhalb der Bibel* (Augsburg, 1928).

25. Carl Bezold, *Kebra Negest: Die Herrlichkeit der Köinige* (Munich, 1905).

26. E. Kautsch, *Die Apokryphen und Pseudepigraphen des alten Testaments: Buch Baruch* (Tubingen), 1900.

27. M.J. (Bin Gorion) Berdyczewski, *Die Sagen der Juden: Von der Urzeit* (Frankfurt, 1913).

28. P. Freuchen, *Book of the Eskimos* (Greenwich, Connecticut, 1961).

29. Erich von Däniken, *Beweise* (Düsseldorf, 1974).

30. Franz Weidenreich, *Apes, Giants and Man* (Chicago, 1946).

31. Denis Saurat, *Atlantis und die Herrschaft der Riesen* (Stuttgart, 1955).

32. *Die Argonauten des Apollonius.*

33. Ibid.

34. Ibid.

35. George Burckhardt, *Gilgamesch; eine Erzählung aus dem alten Orient* (Wiesbaden, 1958).

36. Ibid.

37. *Die Argonauten des Apollonius.*

38. Ibid.

39. Ibid

40. Ibid.

41. Ibid.

42. Ibid.

43. Ibid.

44. Ibid.

45. Ibid.

46. Ovid, *Metamorphosis* (Oxford, 1998).

47. *Die Argonauten des Apollonius.*

48. M.J. (Bin Gorion) Berdyczewski, *Die Sagen der Juden: Juda und Israel* (Frankfturt, 1927).

49. Friedrich Spiegel, *Avesta: die heiligen Schriften der Parsen*, (Leipzig, 1852).

50. Kurt Aram, *Magie und Zauberei in der alten Welt* (Berlin, 1927).

51. *Die Argonauten des Apollonius.*

52. Tripp, *Reclams Lexikon der antiken Mythologie.*

53. Schwab, *Sagen des klassischen Altertums.*

54. R.C. Seaton, *Apollonius Rhodius: The Argonautica* (Cambridge, Mass, 1967).

55. *Die Argonauten des Apollonius.*

56. Ibid.

57. Ibid.

58. Emile Delage and Vian, Francis, *Apollonius de Rhodes: Argonautiques, Tome III, Chant IV* (Paris, 1981).

59. Emile Delage and Vian, Francis, *Apollonius de Rhodes: Argonautiques, Tome II, Chant III* (Paris, 1980).

60. Reinhold Glei and Natzel-Glei, Stephanie, *Apollonius von Rhodos: Das Argonautenepos, Vol. I* (Darmstadt, 1996).

61. Ibid, Vol. II, Book 3 and 4.

62. René Roux, *Le Problème des Argonautes: Recherches sur les Aspects Religieux de la Légende* (Paris, 1949).

63. Christine Pellech, *Die Argonauten: eine Weltkulturgeschichte des Altertums* (Frankfurt, 1992).

64. *Die Argonauten des Apollonius.*

65. Jörg Dendl, *Das Däniken-Register* (Berlin, 1994).

66. Ulrich Dopatka, *Lexikon der ausserirdischen Phänomene,* (Bindlach, 1992).

67. Ibid.

68. Ulrich Dopatka, *Kontakt mit dem Universum* (CD-ROM).

69. Peter Krassa, *Als die gelben Götter kamen* (Munich, 1973).

Chapter 2

1. Erich von Däniken, *Der Gotter-Schock* (Munich, 1992).

2. Erich von Däniken, *The Return of the Gods* (Element Books, 1997).

3. Ernst Curtius, *Griechische Geschichte* (Berlin, 1857).

4. Josef Feix (Editor), *Herodot: Historien, Vol. II* (Munich, 1988).

5. Ibid.

6. Ibid.

7. Michael Rostovzeff, *Geschichte der alten Welt* (Wiesbaden, 1941).

8. Hermann Bengtson, *Griechische Geschichte von den Anfängen bis in die Römische Kaiserzeit* (Munich, 1950).

9. von Däniken, *Return of the Gods*, pages 79–82.

10. Otto Apelt, *Platon: Sämtliche Dialoge. Band VII, Gesetze* (Hamburg, 1922) (translation of this passage, from the German, by MBarton).

11. Ibid.

12. Ibid.

13. M. L. West, *Hesiod's Theogony* (Oxford, 1966).

14. Heinrich Voss, *Hesiod's Werke und Orpheus der Argonaut* (Vienna, 1817).

15. Ibid.

16. Albert von Schirnding, *Hesiod—Theogonie: Werke und Tage,* (Munich and Zurich, 1991).

17. Voss, *Hesiod's Werke und Orpheus der Argonaut.*

18. Walter Marg, *Hesiod. Sämtliche Gedichte. Theogonie, Erga, Frauenkatologe* (Zurich and Stuttgart, 1970).

19. Voss, *Hesiod's Werke und Orpheus der Argonaut.*

20. Ibid

21. Pratāpacandra Rāya, *The Mahabharata,* (Calcutta, 1888).

22. James B. Pritchard, *Ancient Near Eastern Texts Relating to the Old Testament* (Princeton, 1955).

23. Romesh C. Dutt, *The Ramayana and The Mahabharata* (London, 1910)

24. Georg Burckard, *Gilgamesch, eine Erzählung aus der alten Welt* (Wiesbaden, 1958).

25. Nath Manmatha Dutt, *The Ramayana* (Calcutta, 1891).

26. Hermann Jacobi, *Das Ramayana* (Bonn, 1893).

27. Schirnding, *Hesiod—Theogonie: Werke und Tage.*

28. Otto Apelt, *Platon: Sämtliche Werke. Dialoge* (Hamburg, 1922) (translation of this passage, from the German by M Barton).

29. Alfred Jeremias, *Handbuch der altorientalischen Geisteskultur: Astronomie und Astrosophe* (Berlin and Leipzig, 1929).

30. Ibid.

31. Emil Kautzsch, *Die Apokryphen und Pseudpigrapgen des Alten Testaments, Buch Henoch, Band II* (Tübingen, 1900).

32. Adolf Wahrmund, *Diodor von Sizilien, Geschichts-Bibliothek, Book I* (Stuttgart, 1866).

33. Erich von Däniken, *Die Augen der Sphinx* (Munich, 1991).

34. Karl Florenz, *Japanische Mythologie* (Tokyo, 1901).

35. Léon Feer, *Annales du Musée Guimet: Extraits du Kandjour* (Paris, 1883).

Chapter 3

1. H. Hitzig and Blumner, H., *Pausanius* (3 volumes) (Berlin and Leipzig, 1911).

2. Louis E. Lord, *The Pyramids of Argolis* (Athens [no date given]).

3. In *New Scientist*, no 2101/1997.

4. Evi Melas, *Tempel und Stätten der Götter Griechenlands* (Cologne, 1977).

5. Ibid.

6. Unless, of course, the bull was a god!

7. Anna Michailidou, *Knossos* (Athens, 1986).

8. Hans Georg Wunderlich, *Wohin der Stier Europa trug* (Reinbek bei Hamburg, 1972).

9. Ralf Sonnenberg, "Das Ratsel der Magazine," in *Kosmische Spuren* (Munich, 1989).

10. Erich von Däniken, *Wir alle sind Kinder der Götter* (Munich, 1987).

11. Carl Bezold, *Kebra Negest: Die Herrlichkeit der Köinige* (Munich, 1905).

12. Marib in the Yemen.

13. Gaius Plinius Secundus, *Die Naturgeschichte Volumes II and III*, edited by G. C. Wittstein, (Leipzig, 1881).

14. Ibid.

15. James B. Pritchard, *Solomon & Sheba* (London, 1974).

16. A. Sulzbach, *Targum Scheni zum Buch Esther* (Frankfurt, 1920).

17. Derek de Solla Price, *Gears from the Greeks. The Anticythera Mechanism: A Calendar Computer from 80 BC* (Philadelphia, 1974).

18. Ibid.

19. Lutz Gentes, *Die Wirklichkeit der Götter: Raumfahrt im frühen Indien* (Munich and Essen, 1996).

20. Bernhard Carra de Veaux, *L'abrégé des merveilles* (Paris, 1898).

21. Al-Mas'udi, *Bis zu den Grenzen der Erde* (Tübingen and Basle, 1978).

22. Arthur Christensen, *L'Iran sous les Sassanides* (Copenhagen, 1944).

23. Manfred Lurker, *Lexikon der Götter und Damonen* (Stuttgart, 1984).

24. Josef Feix (Editor), *Herodot: Historien, Vol. I* (Munich, 1988).

25. Ibid.

26. Ibid.

27. Al-Makrizi, *Das Pyramidenkapitel in Al-Makrizi's 'Hitat,'* translated into German by Erich Graefe (Leipzig, 1911).

28. Jacques Lacarriere, *Als die Saulen noch standen: Spaziergange mit Pausanias in Griechenland* (Berlin, 1991).

29. "Göttliche Dienste" in *Der Spiegel* no 2 1/1997.

30. Manfred Barthel, *An den Gestaden der Götter* (Dusseldorf, 1989).

31. Erich von Däniken, *Prophet der Vergangenheit* (Dusseldorf, 1979).

32. Ewald Grether, *Theorieheft Planimetria, Part* 2 (no publisher/date given).

33. Theophanias Manias, *Die geometrisch-geodätische Triangulation des altgriechischen Raumes* (Athens, 1970).

34. *La triangulacion geometria-geodesica del espacio de la antigua Grecia* (Madrid, 1971).

35. Theophanias Manias, *The Invisible Harmony of the Greeks* (Athens, 1969).

36. Fritz Rogowski, "Tennen und Steinkreise in Griechenland" in *Mitteilungen der Technischen Universität Braunschweig*, Braunschweiger Hochschulbund, jahrgang V III/2/1973.

37. Ingo Runde, "Griechenlands geheimnisvolle Geometrie" in *Ancient Skies* II, no 11 (Feldbrunnen, Switzerland, 1987).

38. Otto Apelt, *Platon: Sämtliche Dialoge—Kritias und Timaios* (Hamburg, 1922) (translation of this passage, from the German, by M. Barton).

39. Ibid.

40. Gaius Plinius Secundus, *Die Naturgeschichte Volumes I*, edited by G. C. Wittstein, (Leipzig, 1881).

41. Otto Apelt, *Platon: Sämtliche Dialoge. Band VII, Gesetze* (Hamburg, 1922) (translation of this passage, from the German, by M. Barton).

42. F. Schleiermacher, *Platons Werke:Dritter Teil, erster Band* (Berlin, 1828).

43. O. Neugebauer, *The Exact Sciences in Antiquity,* (Rhode Island, 1970).

44. Jean Richter, *Geographie Sacree du Monde Grec* (Paris, 1983).

45. Berthold Laufer, "The Prehistory of Aviation" in *Field Museum of Natural History, Anthropological Series, Vol. XVIII, No. 1.* (Chicago, 1928).

46. Dileep Kumar Kanjilal, "Fliegende Maschinen im alten Indien" in *Habe ich mich geirrt?* (München 1985).

47. Carl Bezold, *Kebra Negest: Die Herrlichkeit der Köinige* (Munich, 1905).

48. Ibid.

49. Ibid.

50. Ibid.

51. Ibid.

52. Ibid

Chapter 4

1.   Homer, *Odyssey*, translated into German by Anton Weihier (Munich, 1955).

2.   Ibid.

3.   Ibid.

4.   Homer, *Ilias*, translated (into German) by Hans Rupé (Munich, 1961).

5.   Armin Wolf and Wolf, Hans-Helmut, *Die wirkliche Reise des Odysseus* (Munich and Vienna, 1990).

6.   Rudolf Stiege, "Eine Schrift, die Zeichen setzt" in *Berliner Illustrierte Zeitung* 13/14 September 1997.

7.   Will Durant, *Die Geschichte der Zivilisation: Das Leben Griechenlands* (Bern, [no date given]).

8.   Birgit Brandau, *Troia: Eine Stadt und ihr Mythos* (Bergisch Gladbach, 1997).

9.   Eberhard Zangger, *Atlantis: eine Legende wird entziffert* (Munich, 1992).

10. "Wegweiser nach Utopia" in *Der Spiegel* no 20/1992.

Chapter 5

1. Otto Apelt, *Platon: Sämtliche Dialoge—Kritias und Timaios* (Hamburg, 1922)

2. Ibid. The author would like to thank the Felix Meiner publishing company in Hamburg for permission to reproduce this version. (Translator's note: the English is a translation of the same version.)

3. Ibid.

4. Ibid.

5. Ibid.

6. Ibid.

7. H.R. Stahel, *So entstand Atlantis* (Zurich, 1980).

8. Otto Apelt, *Platon: Sämtliche Dialoge—Kritias und Timaios* (Hamburg, 1922)

9. Ibid.

10. *Die Argonauten des Apollonius* (Zurich, 1779).

11. Josef Feix, *Herodot: Historien, IV. Buch* (München, 1988).

12. *Aristoteles: De mundo—von der Welt* (Leipzig, 1829).

13. Eberhard Zangger, *Atlantis: eine Legende wird entziffert* (Munich, 1992).

14. Josef Feix, *Herodot: Historien, I. Buch* (München, 1988).

15. Ibid.

16. Angelos Galanopoulos and Bacon, Edward, *Die Wahrheit über Atlantis* (Munich, 1996).

17. Jörg Dendl, *Platons Atlantis-Mythos, Forschung und Kritik* (Berlin, 1996).

18. John Luce, *The End of Atlantis* (London and New York, 1969).

19. John Luce, *Homer and the Heroic Age* (London, 1975).

20. . *Die Quellen und die literarische Form von Platons Atlantis-Erzfalung*, (Frankfurt, 1978).

21. Herbert E. Wright, "Gletscher, Ansteigen des Meeresspiegels und Flutkatastrophen!" in *Atlantis : Mythos, Rätsel, Wirklichkeit?* (Frankfurt, 1978).

22. Fritz Nestke and Riemer, Thomas, *Atlantis: ein Kontinent taucht auf* (Halver, 1988).

23. Heather Lechtmann in *Spektrum der Wissenschaft* August 1984.

Chapter 6

1.   Erich von Däniken, *Die Steinzeit war ganz anders* (Munich, 1991).

2.   Supplement of the *American Journal of Science*, Vol 5, pages 12-13, and Vol 6, pages 332ff.

3.   Byron S. Cummings, "Cuicuilco and the Archaic Culture of Mexico" *Bulletin of the University of Arizona*, Vol IV, 8 November 1933.

4.   Michael Cremo and Thompson, Richard, *Forbidden Archaeology: The Hidden History of the Human Race* (Alachua, Fla., 1993).

5.   Luc Bürgin, *Geheimakte Archdologie* (Munich, 1998).

6.   Paul Kahle, *Die verschollene Columbus-Karte von 1498 in einer türkischen Weltkarte von 1513*, (Berlin and Leipzig, 1933).

7.   Arlington H. Mallery, *New and Old Discoveries in Antarctica*, Georgetown University Forum of the Air, August 26, 1956.

8.   Ibid.

9.   Charles H. Hapgood, *Maps of the Ancient Sea Kings: Evidence of Advanced Civilization in the Ice Age* (Philadelphia and New York, 1965).

10.   Ibid.

11.   Ibid.

12.   Ibid.

13.   Ibid.

14.   Emilio Spedicato, *Apollo Objects Atlantis and other Tales: A Catastrophical Scenario for Discontinuities in Human History* (University of Bergamo, 1995).

15.   Joachim Rittstieg, "Aztlan = Atlantis" in *Mensch und Techik* booklet 4/1992.

16.   Linda Schele and Freidel, D., *Die unbekannte Welt der Maya* (Munich, 1991).

17.   Peter Fiebag, "Die Grabplatte von Palenque und ihre symbolische Aussage" in *Fremde aus dem All* (Munich, 1995).

18.   Eckhardt, Rudolf, "Der Mythos von der aztekischen Lade—Kulturhistorischer Hintergrund und Möglichkeiten einer Suche" in *Das Erbe der Gotter* (Munich, 1997).

19. Diego Durán, *Historia de las Indias de Nueva España e islas de la Tierra Firme* (Mexico, 1984).

20. Spedicato, *Apollo Objects Atlantis and other Tales: A Catastrophical Scenario for Discontinuities in Human History.*

21. Johannes Fiebag, "Die Frage nach Atlantis" in Ancient Skies, no 1/1989.

22. "Schreckens-Szenario eines Asteroiden-Einschlags" in *Die Welt am Sonntag* January 11, 1998.

23. "Wandertrieb im Blut" interview with the molecular geneticist Peter Forster about the prehistoric settlements of America, in *Der Spiegel* no 3/1997.

24. "Ein riesiger Stein rast zur Erde" in *Die Welt* March 13, 1998.

25. Peter Ripota, "In 30 Jahren beginnt die neue Eiszeit" in *PM-Magazine* no 6/1998.

A Final Word on Atlantis

1. L. Sprague de Camps. *Lost Continents* (New York, 1954).

2. Otto Apelt, Platon: *Sämtliche Dialoge. Kritias und Timaios.* (Leipzig, 1922).

3. Josef Feix, *Herodot: Historien, I1. Buch* (München, 1988).

4. Ralph L. Roys, *The Book of Chilam-Balam of Chumayel* (Washington, 1933).

5. Eugen Craine and Reindorp, Reginald, *The Codex Pérez and the Book of Chilam Balam of Maní* (Norman, Okla., 1979).

6. Charles-Etienne Brasseur de Bourbourg, *Histoire des nations civilisées du Mexique et de L'Amérique-Centrale, Tome I – VI* (Paris 1857–1859).

7. Ibid.

8. Ibid.

9. Ibid.

10. Leonhard Schultze-Jena, *Popol vuh, das heilige Buch der Quiché-Indianer von Guatemala* (Stuttgart and Berlin, 1944).

11. Ibid.

12. Bernardino de Sahagún, *Wahrsagerei, Himmelskunde und Kalender der alten Azteken* (Stuttgart, 1950) (Translated by Leonhard Schultze-Jena).

13. Ibid.

14. Ibid.

15. Erich von Däniken, *History is Wrong.* (Franklin Lakes, N.J., 2009).

16. Erich von Däniken, *Twilight of the Gods.* (Pompton Plains, N.J., 2010).

17. Otto H. Muck, *Alles über Atlantis* (Düsseldorf, 1976).

18. Maud Worcester Makemson, *The Book of the Jaguar Priest* (New York, 1951).

19. Letter from Prof. Dr. Gebhardt to Erich von Däniken on November 29, 1972. EvD Archive No. 0238, ECON-Dokumentation.

20. Dr. Heather Lechtman in *Spektrum der Wissenschaft* August 1984

Index

About the Author

Born on April 14th, 1935, in Zofingen, Switzerland, Erich von Däniken was educated at the College St. Michel in Fribourg, where he was already occupying his time with the study of the ancient holy writings. While managing director of a Swiss 5-star hotel, he wrote his first book, *Chariots of the Gods*, which was an immediate best-seller in the United States, Germany, and later in 38 other countries. He won instant fame in the United States as a result of the television special *In Search of Ancient Astronauts*, which was based on the book. His books have been translated into 32 languages and have sold 63 million copies worldwide. In a more recent offering, *Twilight of the Gods: The Mayan Calendar and the Return of the Extraterrestrials*, he meticulously investigates the mysteries surrounding the Mayan calendar, its amazing connection to the Ancient Astronaut Theory, and tantalizing information on the extraterrestrials' prophetic return to Earth.

From his books, two full-length documentary films have been produced, *Chariots of the Gods* and *Messages of the Gods*. As of this writing, the History Channel is producing another 15 episodes of the extremely successful series *Ancient Aliens*, of which Giorgio A. Tsoukalos, of the Center for Ancient Astronaut Research and publisher of *Legendary Times Magazine*, serves as consulting producer. Season 1 and Season 2 are currently on reruns.

Of the more than 3,000 lectures which Erich von Däniken has given in 25 countries, more than 500 were presented at universities. Fluent in four languages, Erich von Däniken is an avid researcher and a compulsive traveler, averaging 100,000 miles each year to remote spots of the globe. This enables him to closely examine the phenomena about which he writes. Erich von Däniken is a member of the Swiss writers association, the German writers association, and the International PEN Club.

He was awarded with an honorary doctorate degree by the La Universidad Boliviana. He received the Huesped Illustre award from the cities of Ica and Nazca in Peru. In Brazil he received the Lourenço Filho award in Gold and Platinum, and in Germany he was awarded with the Order of Gordon Bleu du Saint Esprit (together with the German astronaut Ulf Merbold). In 2004, he was awarded the Explorers Festival prize.

In 1998, Erich von Däniken cofounded the Archaeology, Astronautics, and SETI research society (AASRS), which publishes the English journal *Legendary Times*, reporting on the latest research in the paleo-SETI field. In 2003, he opened his "Mysteries of the World" theme park in Interlaken, Switzerland, which still fascinates visitors with his research into the various mysteries of the world, including paleo-SETI and the Ancient Astronaut Theory.

Today, Erich von Däniken lives in the small mountain village of Beatenberg in Switzerland (40 miles from Berne, above the city of Interlaken). He has been married to Elisabeth Skaja since 1960. He has one daughter, Cornelia (born 1963), and two grandchildren. Von Däniken is an amateur chef and a lover of Bordeaux wines.

Searching For Answers...

Exposed, Uncovered, and Declassified: UFOs & Aliens

Featuring Original Essays by Stanton T. Friedman, Erich von Daniken, Nick Pope, Kathleen Marden, Nick Redfern, Thomas J. Carey, Donald R. Schmitt, Marie Jones & Larry Flaxman, John White,, Jim Moroney, Gordon Chism, and Micah Hanks
EAN 978-1-60163-174-9

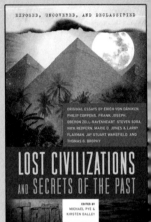

Coming in December

Exposed, Uncovered, and Declassified: Lost Civilizations & Secrets of the Past

Featuring Original Essays by Erich von Daniken, Philip Coppens, Frank Joseph, Oberon Zell-Ravenheart, Steven Sora, Nick Redfern, Marie D. Jones & Larry Flaxman, Adrian Gilbert, Paul von Ward, and Thomas G. Brophy

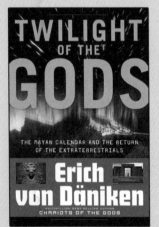

Twilight of the Gods
The Mayan Calendar and the Return of the Extraterrestrials
Erich von Daniken
Foreword by Giorgio A. Tsoukalos
EAN 978-1-60163-141-1
Includes 8-Page-Color Insert

History is Wrong
Erich von Daniken
EAN 978-1-60163-086-5
Includes 8-Page-Color Insert

Visit NewPageBooks.com for more info.
Available Wherever Books Are Sold